FINDING
MY WAY

To your
Success!

Ray

FINDING MY WAY

AND HOW YOU CAN FIND YOURS

RAY PONS

BPS Books
Toronto, Canada
A division of Bastian Publishing Services Ltd.
www.bpsbooks.net

ISBN 978-0-9809231-3-1

Cataloguing in Publication data available from Library and Archives Canada

Cover design: Treefrog Interactive Inc./Tannice Goddard
Typesetting: Greg Devitt, Greg Devitt Design

To my heroes:
business owners, entrepreneurs, sales professionals,
and all self-employed men and women who have
ventured out onto the skinny branches and gone
into business for themselves.

I admire your courage, resilience, drive, determina-
tion, and spirit. I empathize with your occasional
fears, uncertainties, and doubts.

I salute you.

Contents

Acknowledgements

Marva Zulay Castillo, my wife, Queen Bee: You are awesome. Thank God for you. Thank you for not quitting on me. Too many times it would have been easier to do so, and you didn't. Te amo mi vida.

Darien Pons and Patricia Quevedo-Henry: Every parent thinks they have the greatest kids on the planet. They're wrong. I do! Patricia, Darien, les quiero muchisimo.

Mon fils Ruddy Henry: Merci d'aimer ma fille.

To my mom, Alison (Nana): Thank you for loving me always, whether I deserved it or not. And for being an example to all that finding your way is possible even when going it alone.

To Christine and Geoff, Bradley and Laura (the Pleavins), to Jean Francois and Benjamin Coley, Ruben Castillo, Marlene and Francesco, Lilia and Muriel, and the rest of the whole fam-damily in Canada, England, and Venezuela: Thank you for all the love and the laughter.

To Bob Gray, CSP, HoF, awesome speaker and even more awesome man: Cheers mucka!

To Dan Murphy and all of the folks at The Growth Coach: Thanks for the process, the focus, and the accountability. And to my professional family at Rockhurst University, National Seminars: Thank you.

To Toastmasters International, especially the good people at Towns of York Toastmasters in Aurora, Ontario: Your program and your encouragement helped me recognize and develop some God-given talents to maximum impact and gain a general love of learning.

To the Lumpin' Cup boys: Thanks for letting me (Amazin') into the group.

To Judy Suke, my writing coach, Sean Stephens at Treefrog, and everyone who encouraged me to write this book: I am grateful for your interest and your confidence. You have helped me enormously, more than you could ever imagine.

And to all who expressed their doubts: I thank you also, for giving me a discipline and determination that I otherwise might not have had. To Mrs. Mackenzie and Mr. Pons, in particular: You were both wrong—but thanks anyway.

And finally to God, to whom all glory belongs: *The greatest gratitude goes to you.*

God never gives you any hardship without also giving you the strength to deal with it. Some days I do wish that He didn't think I could handle quite so much. But most days I am able to see His will and His work and His purpose in all that I do.

Prologue

Life was easy and life was good. Predictable. Bills paid, twelve handicap, couple of bucks in the hip pocket, sexy missus, two great kids, nice house.

Doesn't it seem that just when you have found your way, or at the very least, believe that you're in the process of finding your way, life gives you a swift, severe kick in the butt?

Life can go from awesome to gruesome in no time flat.

Finding your way is never easy.

It took me several starts and stops and there may be many more for me in the future.

People have asked me, "What is the purpose of this book?" That is one terrific question. My response is always this: "I think of myself as one lost soul, struggling to find his way in business and in life, by helping other people to find their way in business and in life. This book is one way of doing this."

My hope is that you will be truly engaged in what I have written here, in order to discover, through my experiences, how you can find *your* way in *your* work and in *your* life.

1

MRS. MACKENZIE
AND
MR. PONS

In the fall of 1973, I left mother England for Canada. I had no job and no connections and knew no one. I had the grand sum of fifteen thousand dollars to my name, the proceeds of having sold a house prior to emigrating. Not much capital, literal or metaphorical, with which to begin a new life. But that didn't seem to matter much, because what I did have was a dream—a dream of a better life—and Canada was the land where dreams come true.

I had followed Trudeaumania in Canada for several years and the image of this jet-setting prime minister, Pierre Elliott Trudeau, and his trendy wife, Margaret, was appealing. Getting ahead seemed more likely for me in a country with a young, fun-loving couple as its first family than in fusty old England.

Back in the land of my birth, my best chance to advance had fallen completely flat (more on that later in this chapter), prompting me to believe that getting ahead meant somebody else had to retire or die. That belief was pure nonsense, of course, which is one of the funny things I've discovered about my beliefs: I can easily believe what I believe, whether it makes any sense or not.

Believing that I was never going to get very far, very quickly, in England, and on little more than a whim, I'd gotten my immigration papers, sold everything, and now was sitting on a 747 jumbo jet at the Manchester airport, scheduled to leave for the Great White North.

As the plane lumbered into position for takeoff to Toronto, a leap that was to launch me into a new life, I felt not only the usual tension caused by an unexpressed fear of flying, but also anxiety that my move could prove to be a colossal mistake.

Intellectually, I was a man with a dream. Emotionally, I was merely a dreamer. Sure, I had a dream, like Martin Luther King Jr., one of the icons of my youth. Unlike my icon, however, my dream was not much more than a fantasy.

Was I just one of the many eager, well-intentioned folks trying to strike it rich in some foreign land only to return, a few months or a year later, tail between his legs, loaded down with excuses why things just didn't work out? Was I just another wannabe?

Even though I was only twenty-three years old, I had already learned many times over that a dream, even a keen, fervent, and vibrant dream, can oh so frequently and quickly, in the harsh actuality of the real world, turn into a nightmare of failed goals, shattered dreams, and unfulfilled hopes. I knew that burning desires often flicker out into unachieved objectives, that ardent aspirations fizzle into unfulfilled longing. At my tender age, I had already learned, and learned well, not to expect too much.

How does this happen? How does youthful drive—the very essence of hope—so easily, almost effortlessly, become disappointment, disillusionment, and disenchantment? And how is it that this loss of hope, in turn, can almost inexorably lead to despair and a mindset of mediocrity?

Two experiences, burned deep into my memory bank, illustrate my point. They weighed heavily on me as I sat in smoking section, seat 23F, waiting for takeoff. Allow me to introduce you to Mrs. Mackenzie and Mr. Pons.

Mrs. Mackenzie was not one of my favorite teachers, not by a long shot.

The setting was Pooltown Primary School, Ellesmere Port, near Chester, where I spent the years from ages four through ten. Mrs. Mackenzie was my homeroom teacher in my first through third years of school.

She had told me, variously and frequently:

"Pons, you are a troublemaker."

"No good is going to come of you."

"You won't amount to much."

At the time, and for many years to come, I didn't realize that I was buying into her negative impressions and forecasting.

Did Mrs. Mackenzie intentionally want to teach me that I was no good? Did she intentionally mean to give me a negative impression of myself that would prove a problem to surmount? Probably not. But that didn't mean her lessons weren't being learned.

Mrs. Mackenzie was your typical overworked, overwhelmed teacher during the early years of the baby boom generation. Strict rules, unquestioned compliance, and intimidation were the tools she used to control my class of around forty students.

As wide as she was tall, she was a little younger than God, having all of His power and severity but none of His compassion. Even the playful, good-natured shenanigans that are typical of exuberant children in their early years of school were seen by Mrs. Mackenzie as wanton disobedience requiring immediate discipline.

I recall on one occasion being summoned with the ear-piercing shriek, "Pons! Come here this instant!" I approached her desk in the deafening silence that always followed one of Mrs. Mackenzie's banshee outbursts. My mind was fearful. What had I done? I knew that all eyes were on me and that all ears, as well as some mouths, were wide open, in anticipation of what was going to happen.

"What are you doing, Pons?" she said, one painful syllable at a time.

Not knowing the desired response, I volunteered the only thing that came to mind.

"Nothing, Mrs. Mackenzie."

Mrs. Mackenzie glowered at me. "I'll ask again." Her tone of voice was low and threatening, her gaze fierce, her displeasure evident. But the cause of her discomfort remained a complete mystery to me. "Pons … what are you doing?"

"Nothing, Miss."

My tormentor's brow knotted tighter. Her eyes became slits. She stood up, picking up her ruler.

The school ruler was part of each student's welcome package, given to them during registration on their first day of school: a plain twelve-inch wooden ruler with *Pooltown Primary School* embossed on the beveled side. Clear instructions were given to each new arrival about this piece of property: "Lose it and another will be provided only upon payment of an extra charge of two and six-pence. In case you do lose it, put your name on it."

Until I saw this one brandished in Mrs. Mackenzie's hand, I hadn't realized that teachers were also given their own school ruler.

Mrs. Mackenzie navigated her sizeable bulk into a position that only increased her threatening presence. She was now towering above me, hands on hips, bending to put her face only inches from my downcast eyes. My attention was drawn to her right hand, which gripped the ruler.

I noticed that her ruler was distinguished from the hundreds of others in the school by the label "Mrs. Mackenzie" written in permanent marker on the wood of the flat reverse side.

Isn't it strange how the mind works? Even in this moment of fear, mine skittered off on a thoughtful quest. Why would she write her name on her ruler? I know … she doesn't trust herself any more than she trusts us. Why else put her name on a ruler? She expects, at some time, to lose it! And to protect herself against her own carelessness, to provide a means for its return when she eventually does lose it, she has dutifully written her name, in tidy schoolteacher penmanship, directly and permanently onto the ruler, thus saving the penalty fee of two and sixpence.

Then my mind switched focus. Why had she picked up her ruler? She couldn't lose the darn thing while telling me off, and nobody was about to steal it while she was in the room.

I knew the answer, but I didn't want to believe what I knew.

"I will ask you once more, and once more only, Pons. What - are - you - doing?"

The room was church-quiet.

"Well?"

Finally I came up with nothing better than the twice-repeated answer: "Nothing, Miss, I wasn't doing nothing."

Whack!

The ruler made crisp, loud contact with my left leg, leaving a red welt at the point of impact, exactly one inch wide and causing me to jump back in surprise. The welt contained a visible imprint: ооႱ, the first three letters of the school name, in reverse.

The ruler stung my confidence far more than it stung my leg.

Instinctively I lashed out, not with my hands, but with my words:

"What was that for?"

"Don't you use that tone of voice with me, Pons. You know what that was for."

"No I don't."

"Oh yes you do."

"No I don't! No. No. No I don't." I thought yelling would hide the fact that I was crying.

And then, in one moment of pure fury, I shouted in a shrill, clear voice, "I hate you!"

The fierce gaze became fiercer. Evident displeasure became even more evident. The eyes that one nanosecond earlier were narrow slits, now were opened so wide that they bulged.

"What did you say?"

Having let off most of my anger, and knowing that you can never say "I hate you" to a teacher and get away with it, I became motionless and mute, with the exception of an occasional sniff to stop tears-induced snot from dripping onto my upper lip.

Mrs. Mackenzie finally broke the silence. "How dare you, Pons? How dare you? Who - do - you - think - you - are? You've got a big mouth and a bad attitude."

Finger-pointing was now added. "Why, I've a good mind to … You'd better learn how to behave, and show respect to your elders, especially to me, your teacher. You've got a real chip on your shoulder. You better knock that chip off your shoulder, Pons, or you'll never amount to much."

Finger-pointing advanced to shoulder-poking. "You know what, Pons? You are *never* going to amount to much. Never! You hear me, Pons? Never! Now go to the headmaster's study. Now!"

Mrs. Mackenzie thrust a hastily scribbled note into my trembling hand and barked out a curt "Dismissed!"

To this very day, I have no idea what caused her fury.

Isn't it strange how childhood successes, over time, become vague, fuzzy memories, while childhood moments of pain become all the clearer? I know for a fact that I'm not the only person who has carried this kind of baggage into adulthood.

The second person who had caused me to doubt myself was Mr. Pons.

This memory was considerably more recent. It had taken place less than a month earlier and involved one of my childhood heroes, Uncle Alan, my dad's brother.

From as early as I could remember, I had considered Uncle Alan everything that I wanted to become when I grew up. Good looking, charismatic, stylish, and rich, he was the living embodiment of success. Did I mention that he was rich?

I was about twenty years old when I'd gone to my first self-help seminar. The motivational speaker asked us whom we would choose to be if we could be anybody in the whole world. That was a no-brainer for me: Uncle Alan.

The speaker then took a couple of hours to tell us that we must never wish to be that person or anyone else—that we were to become only "the magnificent you that you are!" "Become your own hero!" went the spiel. "You have all that it takes to attain greatness. You possess all that it takes to make a positive impact on the world. You are wonderful and incredible."

The speaker was humorous, engaging, and passionate, with a powerful message that made sense to me and in that moment made me feel strong, energized, and unstoppable. However, no matter how enticing the concept was, intellectually, it was hard for me to be convinced, emotionally.

I would have traded places with Uncle Alan in a heartbeat. So much so that I copied his mannerisms, phrases, and personal characteristics. He smoked Dunhill cigarettes—I switched to the same brand. He drank scotch on the rocks—me, too. He was unable to straighten his right arm due to some childhood accident and walked with it cocked at a forty-five-degree angle. So did I, and I considered my walking style most rakish in appearance.

Some years after I attended that first self-help seminar, Uncle Alan offered me a job in his builders' merchant firm in Birmingham. Hallelujah! From the time I was maybe nine or ten years old, I had fantasized about working for—no, working alongside—my hero.

Be careful what you wish for; you just might get it.

Once I actually started working for Uncle Alan, my impression of him changed dramatically. He began a remarkable transformation, all the way from hero to tyrant.

A perfectionist workaholic, with nothing but urgent priorities, Uncle Alan ruled his business with very little carrot and lots of stick. He issued demands bluntly, abruptly, and abundantly. Customers seemed to like his mantra: "The impossible we do right away—miracles take a little longer." However, the staff knew that every such utterance was the precursor of yet more work, more pressure, and more intensity.

Failure to fulfill any one of his unreasonable promises—or in fact making a mistake of any sort—invariably resulted in a public admonition. Veiled threats were common, sarcasm regular, condescension customary. No matter how hard I tried, nothing was good enough. It wasn't long before I became disillusioned and dispirited. My discomfort grew. Over just a few months, I saw that the writing was on the wall and finally admitted to myself that I had to move on.

My getaway was going to go the distance. I started the paperwork for moving to Canada. It didn't take too many weeks to get government approval and documentation. All that remained was to announce my decision, sell up, and make the move. The hardest announcement, of course, was going to be at work.

I had arranged an appointment with my uncle to let him know that because I was leaving the country, I would be leaving the company. I arrived fifteen minutes early for the meeting and paced outside for twelve or thirteen of those minutes, puffing my way through two Dunhills.

Two minutes ahead of the appointed time, I entered the office and announced to the secretary that I had an appointment with

Mr. Pons. The use of "Mr. Pons" was mandatory for all employees, including me—especially me.

When summoned into the inner sanctum, I was greeted with nothing more than, "Good morning, young man. What can I do for you?"

I mumbled and stumbled through some kind of rambling explanation, before finally conveying that I had decided to go to Canada and would be leaving the firm in a couple of months' time.

Years earlier, when he was about my age, Uncle Alan had gone to South Africa and had lived there for fifteen years. I expected some level of support for what I thought he'd see as my similar wanderlust.

All he said was, "Going to Canada. Indeed. Keep me informed. Anything else?"

I completed the logistics for my move in six weeks, two weeks before my final day of work. That left me with time to pack, give away any unwanted stuff, and say all my goodbyes to family and friends.

Then Mr. Pons pounced. He called me into his office and the moment I sat down began peppering me with questions about why I hadn't done this, how it was that I hadn't completed that, where was the report on this customer, that project? Did I really think I could get away with things just because I'd be leaving soon?

I can't remember anything else he said. I do remember sensing very early in the meeting that this was going to be a pivotal day for me. I couldn't put my finger on exactly what was happening, but somehow I knew it wasn't going to be good.

As he spoke, I spotted a check, payable to me, over on the right side of his desk, almost hidden by the telephone cradle. It seemed to be written in an amount equal to the usual two-week pay cycle. Uh oh. Was I about to be sacked?

Long before Mr. Trump, The Donald, made it fashionable to

point the right index finger at someone and issue a crisp, "You're fired," Uncle Alan pointed at me and said, "Your services are no longer required by this company. Clear out your desk."

My heart was beating hard, my body shaking. My mind was racing, my mouth was not. What I wanted to say was, "Why? Why now? Two weeks from now I'm out of here anyway. I'm working my ass off for you, as always, so why now? Why? Why? Damn it!"

What I did say was, "Fair enough."

In this last cruel act, Uncle Alan completed his transformation from hero to villain with finality, closure, and conclusiveness.

When anyone asked how I felt about being fired, I offered a cavalier, "Hey, no big whoop. I'm getting paid for not working. I mean, it's great: more time to party; more time to pack. He may not have meant to, but Uncle Alan sure did me a big favor."

In reality, I was devastated.

As the 747 lifted into the Manchester sky, Mrs. M. and Mr. P. were my invisible seatmates.

FINDING YOUR WAY

- May begin with a seemingly cavalier break from the past and a move into new territory.
- Often involves taking unwanted passengers along for the ride.
- Will include facing the confidence-sapping incidents of your childhood.

"I am convinced that, except in a few extraordinary cases, one form or another of an unhappy childhood is essential to the formation of exceptional gifts." — Thornton Wilder

2

A
NEW
ADVENTURE

The first few days of the new adventure were an escape. I was living with Joan and Kenny Parr, friends of the family who had immigrated some eight or nine years earlier.

Even though we had never met before, Joan and Kenny agreed to let me stay with them until I could find a job and get into my own place. They were fun people and it was a fun time. Just going to the supermarket was fun. I had never seen so much food in one shop.

There were so many simple things involved in the transition into this new country and new continent: learning English all over again (the Canadian version of the English language and its own unique vocabulary); standing on the wrong side of the street to get on a bus; learning the religion of hockey.

I remember watching City TV's *Baby Blue Movie*—*yummy*—eating a plate of this new fast food, Kentucky Fried Chicken—*yummy*—after a boys' night out at the Legion telling jokes and exchanging stories from over 'ome—*boozy*.

But soon enough it was time to turn the dream into reality: It was time to go to work.

After only a couple of weeks in the country, I got a job as a car salesman. The interviewer asked me exactly five questions, none of which was terribly hard to answer. Then, during my response to his fifth question, I mentioned that I'd just arrived from England. He surprised me with, "All righty then. Might as well give a break to a fellow Brit." It turned out that his dad had been an immigrant some forty-five years earlier.

I started the next day—and lasted only two more.

The dealership was a terrific high-end outfit in the Yorkville neighborhood in midtown Toronto. Two or three years later it may have been a great opportunity. But exactly twenty-three days after I arrived in this new country was way too early for a commission–only sales position—especially considering that I knew precisely the square root of squat about selling anything, never mind Alfa Romeos, Porsches, and Ferraris. Three days later I was back pounding the pavement, looking for work.

Four weeks in I'd been through many more interviews— tougher interrogation-style ones—and was again experiencing self-doubts. Instead of thinking, "I have a dream," I again began wondering, "Am I merely a dreamer?"

However, three tense weeks after that, I was offered a job, at Imperial Tobacco. The job was a regular, if somewhat entry-level, sales representative position that required me to visit wholesalers and retailers, put up point-of-sale materials, replace damaged or stale-dated product, and generally represent the company. It was a most decent job with a regular paycheck, good benefits, and favorable perks—a great way to settle into a new country.

Two weeks shy of three mostly uneventful years, I got my first promotion, just after a new president took charge. The newly appointed head honcho had apparently seen something in me that he liked.

President Pierre, once a professional football player, was massive in both build and personality. For him and me to connect seemed unlikely. I was slightly built and more interested in crossword puzzles than gridiron plays. I hadn't arrived in Canada until a full five years after the linebacker's retirement. While I had indeed developed an interest in football, especially ABC's *Monday Night Football* with Howard Cosell and "Dandy" Don Meredith, I was blissfully unaware of my new boss's fame and celebrity.

Even the CFL Grey Cup ring, prominently displayed on President Pierre's right hand—an item of acute influence on the rest of the management group, especially the kiss-up artists—had completely escaped my attention. University ring, Saturday Night Fever ring, Grey Cup ring. They were all the same to me.

I had a noticeable English accent; Pierre's was heavily French-Canadian. I hadn't finished high school; Pierre had a university degree, honors, plus a post-graduate MBA. I lacked confidence; Pierre oozed it.

In spite of all this, we connected.

He had a confidence in my abilities that I didn't have. He saw a future for me that I couldn't yet picture.

Immediately after Pierre took charge, I was put onto what was referred to at the time as the fast track. I was thoroughly enjoying the bigger paycheck, a better company car, and the fancy title of sales training manager, and before long I also began to enjoy the increased visibility of being on the outer rim of the inner circle, with the support of the person at its very center. Before the word became a central part of the vocabulary of business, the president became my mentor and I his protégé.

Before long, the impressionable, uncertain Ray began to take on some of the positive leadership characteristics of Pierre. I was more decisive. I was developing a personal presence. I was displaying a lot more poise and charisma. And I was feeling it.

Even the moniker "Junior" didn't faze me. This was a term

created by Pierre, perhaps as a reflection of his football back-ground, and given to new management appointees. Pierre must have thought the term would be a humbling yet fun way to wel-come the rookies into management, keeping the newly promoted from getting too high an opinion of themselves.

Several of the existing managers, especially those still suffering from the hierarchical influences of the old regime, saw it as a way to keep the new guys in their place.

"Junior, when you go down to the training session, can you get me a coffee from the lunchroom? It's on your way."

"Bring me a Danish when you take a break, would ya, ju-nior?"

"Run two copies for me when you go to the Xerox machine. Okay, junior?"

Whatever the request was, I did it. I acted as if it had never oc-curred to me that a power struggle was taking place. It seemed to me that if the intended victim didn't struggle, the aggressor would soon weary of the sport. I was right.

During management meetings, Pierre stressed the team con-cept of "all must participate," and I did just that. I wasn't restricted by the paradigm of the existing management group, which could be summed up as "find out what the boss thinks and then agree with it." I regularly volunteered my thoughts on the issues being discussed. Despite being inexperienced in how management de-cisions were arrived at, my ideas, even the daftest of them, were received by Pierre with an "Interesting" or "What do da rest of you tink of dat suggestion?"

It wasn't until years later that I realized he asked this question without a clue whether he thought the idea was good or bone-headed.

The more Pierre asked for my ideas, the more security and confidence I gained. I moved from Junior to Good Guy fairly easily, without making outright enemies or attracting blatant competitors. My future was full of potential.

Which is why it was so surprising to everyone when I quit. And quit I did.

FINDING YOUR WAY

- May sometimes involve another person believing in you more than you believe in yourself.
- Is about making choices to respond, not react, to people, things, and circumstances.
- Sometimes means getting off one track and setting out on another.

"In addition to self-awareness, imagination and conscience, it is the fourth human endowment—independent will—that really makes effective self-management possible. It is the ability to make decisions and choices and to act in accordance with them. It is the ability to act rather than to be acted upon ..." — Dr. Stephen Covey

3

❧◉❧

ONTO
THE
SKINNY
BRANCHES

I quit the fast track of management at one of the largest and most profitable multinational corporations in Canada to become, of all things … a life insurance salesman.

Not only was I making a dramatic switch in direction; not only was I making an entry into the ranks of the self-employed; not only was I giving up solid job security to become a commissioned salesman, oh no, in the grand scheme of things I was doing something much worse: I was becoming a commissioned *life insurance* salesman.

To most everyone, I was crazy. My draw against commissions in my new job was far below half of my previous salary. No company car. No benefits. No pension plan. No expense account. No perks. No security.

The truth was that while on the surface I had seemed content at Imperial Tobacco, and to most everyone else I had a good job and a good future, I had developed a nagging sense of doubt. Over time the doubt became discomfort. Before long the job discomfort became greater than the job security.

About a year earlier, my father had passed away after a fierce yet fairly brief battle with cancer. The cancer was first noticed on a CAT scan of his brain, part of a battery of tests ordered because of dramatic mood swings and angry outbursts that had punctuated his behavior over the previous several weeks. He'd gone from an easy-going joke teller to a ticked-off, angry brute. The tumor explained the behavioral change.

Next, a shadow was seen on an x-ray of his lungs. The doctors deemed that the cancer had started in the lung and then spread to the rest of his body, resulting in the brain tumor. No treatment would be effective. The cancer had advanced too far.

The cause of the cancer was cigarettes.

My dad, a "social smoker" since just about forever, had become part of the ever-growing statistics on the negative effects of smoking: the very same statistics that I had been competing against at the tobacco company.

In my role as sales training manager, my focus had been to train new sales representatives in how to deal with all of the "false and scurrilous allegations of the anti-smoking radicals." I trained them to follow the tried and true procedures that would balance the "completely unfounded accusations of the health nuts and mis-guided advocacy groups." I taught new reps a variety of slogans and sayings designed to counteract the assertions of those on the other side.

"Smoking is a choice made in a free society by responsible adults."

"Everything in moderation."

"We don't encourage anybody to smoke. We just want people who are already smokers to choose one of our brands when they buy."

This part of the training was easy and enjoyable. I wasn't just trotting these phrases out in rote manner; I wholeheartedly believed them. I truly did view the issue as one of freedom and rights. I ardently defended people's right to choose.

"Even if smoking is harmful, and there's no hard evidence to suggest that it is, people must never give up their rights to decide for themselves what they want to do with their own bodies, especially when it doesn't harm anybody but themselves."

The allegations of advocacy groups, to my mind, were the thin end of the wedge. Failure to defend the rights of smokers would be the precursor of the end of the freedoms and rights of all Canadians, indeed of all people everywhere.

It was heady stuff.

Heady stuff, that is, until my dad's diagnosis, followed by his agonizing, painful death.

The various catch phrases, slogans, and jingles no longer fit as comfortably as before, and when you're trying to train others to believe in something, you had better believe in it yourself. Selling tobacco became very difficult for me. I needed to be doing something else. As for what that something else might be, that was a complete mystery.

I was listlessly working on something or other in my office when I got a call from a man who worked for Canada Life: an innocuous two-minute telephone call that would change my life.

"Ray—may I call you Ray?—my name is Roger Macmillan, my friends call me Roger. I'm a sales manager with Canada Life and I've been referred to you by a good client of mine. Is now a good time for us to speak?"

"About what, Roger?"

"Ray, I'm calling about an exciting career opportunity. It's a career opportunity that someone with your experience in sales just might find of interest. Or it may be of no interest whatsoever. I'm calling to ask when would be a good time for us to at least meet and have a bite to eat, so I can fill you in on some of the details. Would Thursday at noon be good, or would Friday at one be better?"

I thought "what the heck" and we arranged a get together.

To this day I still can't recall whether it was the Thursday or Friday when we met. What I do recall is the swift transition from the sandwich lunch in Roger's nondescript office to the plush surroundings of the agency manager, Tony Lawes. This office dripped with power, prestige, and luxury. Dimmed lighting highlighted the impressive art on the walls. I was welcomed to sit on a rich burgundy couch with that seductive aroma of new leather. Tony's massive oak desk glistened and at its corner stood a pewter bust of Winston Churchill in his world-famous hands-on-hips pose, cigar clamped between gritted teeth.

Even more impressive was the man in the office. Tony was impeccably groomed, the essence of dress for success. His ability to communicate was equally stylish. For an hour I sat transfixed while being charmed and challenged, prodded and poked, by a series of carefully crafted statements about personal meaning, vision, fulfillment, and purpose. These were followed with comments about personal independence, financial wealth, and the material trappings of success.

Tony wasn't so much someone you immediately liked as someone you instantly respected. He was often described as resolute, determined, and unrelenting—or, less graciously, as intimidating, aloof, and unfeeling.

The meeting concluded with a direct question: "Everyone says they want to be successful, Mr. Pons. Very few are willing to actually pay the price to make it happen. The question I ask you is this: Are you one of the few who are willing to pay the price?"

Internally, I responded, "I'm not sure." To Tony, I said, "I think I am."

"Time will tell, Mr. Pons. Time will tell."

Roger was summoned to retrieve the candidate and continue the recruitment process.

When I'd arrived at the office, I was expecting little more than a chat and a free lunch. Now, only an hour or so later, I was intrigued, to the point of being enthusiastic. I was ready to do just about whatever they required to determine if a career in life insurance was right for me.

Three short yet intense months later, I had completed all of the pre-contract requirements and demands. I had talked to many of the agents in the branch—mostly those who were doing well, of course. I sponged up as much information as possible, asking questions, probing to get some kind of inkling of whether this was the way for me to go.

In late September, it was time for me to decide. Was I to become a career agent in the Toronto branch of Canada Life?

I was frightened and excited, hesitant and eager, uncertain and won over. I hemmed and hawed for several days, second-guessed myself repeatedly, and then finally made the decision. I was entering the ranks of the self-employed.

A Chinese proverb states, "If we do not change our direction, we are likely to end up where we are headed." Another proverb states, "It is better to run back than run the wrong way." I had come to see that I was on the wrong path going the wrong way. Time to change direction.

FINDING YOUR WAY

- Sometimes, often, comes down to the choices you make.
- Can begin when someone else points an opportunity out to you.
- Can be frightening, accompanied by many doubts and scarce support.

"The last, if not the greatest, of the human freedoms: to choose their own attitude in any given circumstance." — Bruno Bettelheim

"It takes great courage to break with one's past history and stand alone." — Marion Woodman

4

WHO
DO YOU
THINK
YOU ARE?

Writing my letter of resignation proved to be a real challenge. It was made particularly difficult by the close relationship I had developed over the previous several months with my boss and mentor Pierre.

On that issue, I need not have worried. When he learned of my decision, he was by far the most supportive of my judgment. He read my letter, placed it deliberately on his desk, looked me in the eye, smiled, and in his charming and personable way said, "New career. I wish you success. You will do well, Ray, very well. Of dat I 'ave no doubt."

It was the last positive comment that I was to hear for quite some time.

My best buddy said, "Are you nuts? Have you lost your mind?"

My wife, whom I thought was supportive, reacted with an indignant, "How dare you do this to me?"

Even my mom expressed doubt. In a transatlantic phone call she said, "Oh son, why would you want to do a silly thing like that when you've already got a real job?"

Isn't it curious how those who know us little often provide the greatest support and encouragement, while those closest to us, those who love us the most, don't hesitate to trample over our heartfelt dreams, desires, and aspirations?

The latter don't mean to deliberately squash our drive and passion. They want to keep us out of harm's way. They don't want to see us experience pain, distress, or disappointment. Their intentions are usually pure. However, it mattered not one iota to me what their intentions were. To me their comments were as clear as Caesar's thumbs down to a defeated gladiator in the coliseum: "You are going to die. You will fail. Whatever are you thinking?"

As positive as I had previously been about working for myself, the unsought counsel revitalized my severe misgivings.

Mrs. Mackenzie once more took up residence in my mind. "Who do you think you are? You know what, Pons, you are never going to amount to much. Never! You hear me, Pons? Never!"

Uncle Alan was once again dismissing me with a flicker of his carefully groomed eyebrow.

But I'd come too far to give up now.

Despite my inner turmoil, I attempted to maintain an appearance of composure and confidence. I was trying hard to ignore the noisy, negative voices of others and hear the quiet, positive voice that was my own. It would be many years later that I would watch the animated feature film *The Land Before Time* and be touched by the mother dinosaur saying to her baby, Littlefoot, with her dying breath, "Let your heart guide you. It whispers, so listen closely."

I had read somewhere that "people don't make right decisions; they make decisions … and work like hell to prove them right."

I'd made a decision, a hard one. Now it was time to work, and work hard, to prove the decision right.

I wasn't so much driven to succeed as to not fail. I wasn't concerned so much with being right as with proving everybody else wrong.

I remember being in my car, returning from a particularly memorable appointment—memorable because of how badly it went—and addressing the dashboard of my car: "I may not make it big, but I am at least going to make it. First I will make it, then I will quit. Damn it! Then and only then will I quit! Double damn it!"

FINDING YOUR WAY

- Means learning to hear your own voice over the roar of the negative voices of others.
- Involves listening hard to hear your whispering heart: going with your passion and trusting your instincts.
- Means making decisions and then working to make those decisions turn out right.

"My basic principle is that you don't make decisions because they are easy; you don't make them because they are cheap; you don't make them because they're popular; you make them because they're right." — Theodore M. Hesburgh

5

JUST
DO
IT

Working hard at my new job was mostly about putting in time and following instructions.

In Tony Lawes' branch, all new agents were required to follow a production system created by a gentleman named Alfred O. Granum. It was drummed into us that adherence to Granum's One Card System would lead to good results.

"We will tell you how to be successful. We will give you a precise, proven system for success that works. It works if you work. If you do what we tell you to do, it isn't a question of if you will be successful, it's a question of how successful you will be. We can tell you exactly what it takes, but it's up to you whether you will do it."

I decided that I would do it.

We were expected to be in the office each day at seven in the morning, and we usually didn't get to leave until well past nine at night. Every aspect of the day was laid out for the new recruits, a combination of product training, professional development, administrative procedures, and most importantly, the sales process, always the sales process. It was a hectic, frenzied, activity-filled time.

Perhaps the most vital part of all this was the emphasis on making telephone calls.

"No one has ever failed when they make twenty calls a day. No one! Twenty calls will have you talk to ten people. Speaking to ten people will yield three appointments, and three appointments will generate one sale and at least two referrals. Twenty – ten – three – one – two. It all starts with the phone calls. Ya gotta make the calls. Make the calls and success will follow. No agent making twenty calls a day has ever failed. Ever!"

Every telephone call made, every dialing of a number, became a dot entered on my daily calendar. If I got to speak to someone, the dot became a check mark. If that someone agreed to meet with me, this was noted with two diagonal lines across the swoop of the check. The numbers game had been developed into a simple system of procedure, process, and routine.

Too doubtful to disagree, and not creative enough to come up with anything else, I worked the One Card System to the letter.

At least one hour per day, every day, was spent on the phone. Some days it was four, five hours, or more. Mind-numbing, terrifying cold calls.

In addition, as long as I was on the draw against commissions—the low but guaranteed paycheck I received every two weeks—it was mandatory that I be in the bullpen at least two evenings per week for two hours of dialing for dollars. This was a time of making telephone calls along with four, five, or six other agents who were also trying to get appointments and doing it in a format of friendly competition.

Each successful call—one that got an appointment—would allow the agent to make an entry beneath his name on a flip chart and then to ring the bell. A school bell had been hung in the bullpen years earlier for just that purpose. I rarely got to ring it.

My telephone stats were way off the expected average. It wasn't rare for me to make sixty, seventy, or eighty calls in a day and speak to only ten, twelve, or fifteen people. Feeling rejected and dejected, I nevertheless kept plugging away.

I was so accustomed to not getting anyone on the other end of the phone that I was unable to follow the prepared Granum script when someone actually answered. More times than not I'd confuse the person as to why I was calling and they'd hang up.

At other times, I accepted the "Sorry, not interested" far too easily.

For me, it took at least twenty or more telephone contacts to get the three appointments that I was supposed to get in ten.

I made enough calls each and every day to consistently get a couple of people to agree to see me. Some of my colleagues thought that my determination was born of a powerful desire to succeed. Little did they know that it was derived from a desire to not fail. "I may not make it big, but I am at least going to make it. First I will make it, then I will quit!"

After a while, my mediocre performance and poor ratios did start to have a positive impact. I was the first of the new agents who no longer depended on the typewritten scripts when calling. I had said each of them so often that I could pull them out of my memory bank almost without thinking. Perhaps that's why my calls began to sound less scripted and more people were agreeing to see me.

However, the meetings with prospective clients went no better than the calls.

Every three meetings were supposed to result in one sale: big sale, medium sale, or little sale. My first five meetings were a wipe-out. This was followed by a sixth meeting without success. Zip, zilch, nada: discouragement squared.

I recited to myself the clichés of the times. They were powerful and solid to some, mindless simplicity to others:

"When the going gets tough, the tough get going."

"Whatever doesn't kill you makes you stronger."

"Successful people do what unsuccessful people won't do."

"Tough times don't last; tough people do."

No matter how many motivational mantras I parroted, the one I went back to time and time again was: "I may not make it big, but I am at least going to make it. First I will make it, then I will quit. Damn it!"

Finally, mercifully, I broke the ice and some sales started trickling in. What I lacked in skill I made up for in effort. The greater the effort, the stronger my confidence. The successes were never big enough, or frequent enough, to generate top-notch confidence, but at least I did start feeling a wee bit stronger.

And the stronger my confidence, the better I was able to persist through my lousy ratios.

I kept making the calls, making the calls, making the calls.

I had survived the first one hundred days! I hadn't failed! While I hadn't yet "made it," I had at least made it to year-end. I wasn't exactly living my dream, but neither had I flamed out.

As the New Year began, everyone started with a clean slate. It was time to take a look at the first one hundred days and then plot out what my goals would be for the year ahead.

FINDING YOUR WAY

- Means taking action.
- Requires you to follow a system.
- Involves taking an honest look at where you are, what you have done, and then committing, learning, to do things better.

"If you act like you know what you're doing, you can do anything you want—except neurosurgery." — John Lowenstein

6

THEN
DO
IT
WELL

Goals give you direction. Goals give you focus. Goals give you motivation.

For me, at that time, goals were a waste of time.

A day-long goal-setting meeting, involving the entire office of the Toronto branch, was a pleasant and meaningless waste of a day. Roger Macmillan and the other managers guided us through the process. We were then expected to continue following the Granum One Card System to make those goals happen. Yeah, right.

I wasn't concerned about making Roger's goals come true. I was concerned about making mine come true: survive, then quit.

However, I kept my cynicism to myself and established a variety of formal goals for the upcoming year.

The New Year proceeded in much the same way as the previous one had ended. I plodded along, working hard and studying hard.

I was beginning to acquire some positive attributes. I was settling into a solid routine, showing fairly good discipline. I kept making the calls. I followed the system. I didn't buck the basic approach.

One thing that did change from the previous year was that I was hanging around a good group of guys. Admittedly, these agents were the B Group of producers, but all of them were eager to join the A Group. Associating with them was having a good influence on me.

Urged on by this B clique, my skills improved. I attended every training seminar and conference within a sixty-mile radius. I listened to self-help tapes while in the car. I watched motivational videos and uplifting TV shows. I read, cover to cover, several manuals of the Million Dollar Round Table annual meeting, paying closest attention to the sections on sales tips, attitude, and motivation.

I tried out new ideas. I asked for advice constantly. I looked for better ways to work. I made the calls, recorded the dots, kept appointments, completed a few sales, and asked for referrals.

Then one of life's momentous events occurred.

For three months I'd been working on my first corporate-owned insurance case, involving a buy-sell agreement for three partners of an anodizing firm, a business that put metal coatings onto a variety of components for heavy machinery and manufacturing equipment. Never before had I met with a potential client more than twice. This case was now heading into the fifth meeting with the clients and at least as many meetings not involving them.

The case had progressed to the point where many of my B Group colleagues and all of the A Group elite were suggesting that I was suffering from big-case-itis: the belief that one large case, one biggie, would pull a struggling agent out of the doldrums. All too often I heard statements like:

"It's a china egg, let it go."

"Get real!"

"It's not going to happen."

"Several singles score more runs than a home run that doesn't leave the park."

Then came a sunny Wednesday in May. After a very exciting sixth meeting with the partners, which had begun early in the afternoon and ended late in the day, I was much closer to where I lived than to the office. But I was way too keyed up to go home.

When I entered the office, I was delighted to see that the bullpen was still filled with agents. We were at the peak of Spring Campaign, one of two sales campaigns held throughout the year, and it was common for agents to work late during these times. During campaigns several bonuses were available. Prizes were there to be had. Personal image and professional prestige were on the line. Everyone's production was much more noticed.

I walked to the production board, doing my best to keep a poker face. My hand was shaking. No kidding. It was shaking for real. I scribbled three numbers onto the board: $1900, $2100, and $3850.

Those numbers reflected that the biggie had been bagged. The china egg had hatched. The home run had cleared the bases.

My meeting that day had resulted in the completion of three applications for corporate-owned, permanent life insurance that would be used to fund a buy-sell agreement of the three partners.

It was only when I finished writing the third number that I realized that the bullpen buzz had fallen silent.

I turned away from the board with an ear-to-ear grin. The buzz returned with explosive immediacy. The congratulations were boisterous.

"Holy crap!"

"Way to go, Ray."

"Outstanding."

If these applications were successfully underwritten, accepted, and placed, my commission would be about $10,000, and then a further $10,000 for the following two years. On this one day, I had had a good month. Hey, not a good month, a good quarter. It was a heck of a lot more income than the draw of a thousand bucks a month that I'd been surviving on for the last several months.

You know what I learned? When you sell policies of this size, forces come to your assistance to get the contracts placed easily, smoothly, and quickly. In record time the contracts were approved, delivered, and settled. I got letters of congratulations from senior executives whom I had never even met. I was talked about at team meetings. I was asked for help. Some of the A Group members said hello to me. Hello!

The plodder had become a thoroughbred.

Instead of being the one who sought advice from other agents, I was asked for advice. I moved out of the bullpen and into an office—a shared office, but an office nonetheless. I moved off the draw into commission-only status.

Funny how your confidence can grow when your bank balance grows.

In my case the growth in confidence was more the result of a smaller credit card balance. The Visa bill in July, showing "Past Due: $0," was as attractive to my eyes as Michelangelo's Venus de Milo, the goddess Aphrodite, or the Playmate of the Month.

Emboldened by my success, I focused a little bit more on the business market. I got a few referrals from the partners I'd just signed up to other business owners and from them to yet others. The system was now working well for me. I was able to do more daytime work and have fewer nighttime appointments. My ratios and general effectiveness improved. More good-sized sales were made.

With a solid year-end push, including one last sale on, of all days, Christmas Eve, I accomplished something that no one could possibly have imagined at the start of the year: I qualified for the previously mentioned Million Dollar Round Table.

This is an independent agent group that requires productivity of at least one million dollars of permanent life insurance in a calendar year, plus certain quality standards and persistency of business. Only two percent of the world's life insurance agents ever qualify, and a mere half of one percent accomplish it in their first year. People were telling me that I was in the half of one percent group.

I reminded them that I'd been in the business for three months of the previous year, but people told me that those days didn't count, not really. They were much too generous and accommodating, but I wasn't going to argue with them. It felt far too good.

From that point my business grew steadily and solidly. Although I was never in the echelon of the true top guns, I was always able to maintain solid numbers.

I was a consistent qualifier for the Round Table four years running. I was a member of one of the premier golf clubs and became a sought-after presenter at industry functions. I was asked to share tips, tactics, and strategies that were helping me build my business. The original goal, "First I am going to make it, then I'll quit," was easily forgotten.

I hadn't planned for success, merely planned not to fail. Yet success had found me anyway.

Life was good. Life was easy. Life was grand. You would think that by now I would know well enough to expect the unexpected. Life and circumstance were once again planning to throw me into a tailspin.

Natalie Goldberg wrote, "Life is not orderly. No matter how we try to make life so, right in the middle of it we die, lose a leg, fall in love, drop a jar of applesauce."

I was about to drop a jar of applesauce.

FINDING YOUR WAY

- Means having goals.
- Is accelerated by hanging around with the right crowd.
- Will sometimes mean nothing more than allowing success to find you.
- Means never getting complacent, not for a moment, not for a second, not for an instant.

"The only thing that makes life possible is permanent, intolerable uncertainty, not knowing what comes next." — Ursula K. Le Guin

7

FASTEN
YOUR
SEAT BELTS

As my business flourished, my personal life floundered. My marriage was in trouble.

I was working long days, leading to detachment and distraction at home. This progressed to tension that became severe and persistent. I guess I figured that if I took care of business, life would take care of itself. It didn't.

Right around the time of our ninth wedding anniversary and the fifth anniversary of my entry into the insurance business, the marriage finally collapsed.

So did my work. Good habits decreased, bad habits increased. Results got worse. Normally respected for my stubborn determination, I was rapidly gaining a reputation for indecision and being distracted and unfocused.

I'd moved away from the Granum One Card System of the agency without ever developing a solid system of my own to replace it. The lack of a system wasn't a problem when sales were coming in. It became a big problem when they ceased.

I drifted aimlessly from one mediocre week to the next.

I couldn't seem to do anything to get out of the blue funk I was in.

Personal feelings of discomfort were exaggerated by the fact that my wife worked just four floors up in the same company. My personal issues seemed to be as well known throughout the office as my drop in production. It was a time of personal and professional turmoil.

It was also a time of prevailing uncertainty for the business in general. The staid, dependable world of life insurance was experiencing market pressures and turbulence: massive product change; dramatic modification of the distribution channels; major cutbacks in support services; increased expenses; reduced compensation.

The pressure reached a high point when I received a commission check for precisely forty-seven cents.

Right around this time, I came to the attention of a reinsurance company. This segment of the insurance world was especially volatile, which resulted in significant staffing changes, especially in sales and marketing.

In this more aggressive, price-driven marketplace, often involving cutthroat competitive business practices, major modifications had to be made. Even the largest, most stable reinsurance companies were losing money, great gobs of money, in unheard of proportions. Treaties no longer sold themselves, at least not at a profit.

An immediate change that would directly affect me was a decision by one of the major reinsurance companies to alter its sales strategy. They decided that in order to thrive, not just survive, they would need to schmooze less and sell more. They decided to focus head office folks—who were previously looking after sales—on technical head office work and establish a genuine sales force to take care of selling. In today's business environment, this may seem rather obvious. At the time, it was a radical shift.

Even in the world of insurance, life insurance salesmen did not have a particularly positive reputation. As for the notion of hiring them into the refined world of reinsurance, well, this would surely cause the traditionalists to balk.

Balk they might; change they did. An executive of a reinsurance firm located just five blocks from my downtown condo knew me from my involvement in various industry functions. He began a conversation with me at one such event that ultimately led to my being offered a position as regional director, sales and marketing. If I took the offer, I would be the company's first real salesman. I jumped at the chance.

My reasons were several: company benefit plan; lots of travel with a hefty expense allowance; plenty of wining and dining; good office location; and a seductive incentive bonus plan. But the most compelling reason was that the position came with a good-sized salary, and, best of all, a guaranteed salary.

Yet, no matter how much I rationalized the reasons for leaving, the core issue wasn't really about moving to new and better circumstances. It was about moving away from bad ones.

I was exhausted. The day-to-day stresses and strains of self-employment, combined with the tensions of divorce and personal readjustment, were proving too much for me to deal with. A job with a guaranteed five-figure income seemed a much easier road to travel.

For the next four years I sold and schmoozed, schmoozed and sold my way across the northeast of the United States, traveling a great deal and growing the book of business from $250 million to $2.4 billion. A ten-times increase in little more than a year. My star was once again in the ascendancy and my confidence had returned.

However, although business was growing in quantum leaps, my income didn't. Financially, I was doing all right, better than all right, but I had bumped up against a very definite income ceiling. I didn't like it. The more the book of business grew, the more my discomfort with my income grew.

Once again I began drifting. Once again I was losing my way, except this time without losing the income. As was the case nine years earlier at Imperial Tobacco, and then again three years earlier at Canada Life, I had quit. However, this time I had somehow contrived to quit and stay.

Each day I would turn up at the office on time and go through the motions of working. I'd attend meetings, call clients, and co-ordinate a variety of tasks and functions to display the illusion that I was actually working. No one seemed to notice the difference between the present illusion and the initial results-oriented reality.

However, a new element entered the mix. While I may have been losing my way in business, I was finding my way in love. Uh oh—mushy stuff follows.

Back about twelve months, when I was in my third year in the reinsurance world, I had met Marva Zulay Castillo, an exciting Latin American lady, born and raised in Caracas, Venezuela. Marva was the proud parent of a precocious nine-year-old ballerina girl, Patricia Quevedo.

Marva quickly pointed out to me, when I was dropping her off after our very first date, that no man would ever come between Patricia and her.

"She's the most important person in the world to me and I just wanted you to know that if ever a choice was necessary between Patricia (charmingly pronounced Patree-see-ya) and some man, well, there wouldn't be any choice. Just wanted you to know. G'night."

A quick kiss to the cheek and she moved indoors to get Patricia ready for bed. I had been summarily dismissed to hook up with the TTC bus headed back downtown. The passengers on the bus must have wondered why I had a goofy grin on my face. I was as taken by Marva's love for her daughter as I had been by Marva herself.

I fell in love with the mother almost instantly and it was no time at all that I became equally as smitten by her infectious, energetic daughter.

A whirlwind romance resulted in marriage less than a year later. I was introduced to the joys of moving from bachelor (self-indulgent bachelor for the most part) to husband and instant parent (step-poppa). It was a fun-filled transition that added meaning to my superficial going-through-the-motions life.

To this point, the "one week in, one week out routine" at work had been exciting and energizing. Getting out of town every other week meant getting out from under the frustrations of office politics and my own office game-playing. Coasting was much easier when not under the scrutiny of a nine to five office workday. Dates were sufficient, obligations few. Life on the road was bartenders and barmaids, discos and casinos, sports and sporting events, wining and dining.

Now that I was a husband and step-poppa, however, life on the road was dreary and tedious. Traveling wasn't something that distanced me from reality; it was something that distanced me from family.

The more my frustrations grew over my travel schedule, the more they grew over my work. The more they grew over work, the more they started to spill over into my home life. And the more I brought them home, the more Marva's impatience was brought home to me.

"If you don't like it, then get out. Do something else," she would say.

"Easy for you to say," was my usual mumbled response.

You see, as the list of "didn't likes" grew larger and my frustrations grew bigger, my confidence became smaller. I was facing head-on the prospect that the only long-lasting solution to my frustration would be a return to self-employment. Which scared the tarpaper out of me.

It was clear that other employee positions would not be that different from the one I already had: same horse, different jockey; same issues, different players; same annoyances, different surroundings.

However, the more I contemplated my predicament, the more I was reminded of the tensions involved in self-employment. I was especially conscious of the financial issues. While I was annoyed that my pay hadn't gone up as much as the business had increased, every two weeks, regular as clockwork, a good-sized deposit hit my bank account. I was making more than most folks I knew while doing less than most of them were expected to do.

And now, as a family man, I had other considerations to take into account beyond whether or not I was happy at my job. Sure, there were no hefty paychecks like the ones from the fat years of my time as an insurance agent, but neither were there the checks for forty-seven cents of the lean times.

My internal voices yammered at me one way and then the other:

"What if you fail again? What if production falls flat like last time?"

"What if you're holding yourself back from unlimited potential?"

It was an emotional roller coaster. I was too timid to leave, but not timid enough to comply. I was too afraid to get out, but not sufficiently afraid to get along. I was too frustrated to give a best effort, but not frustrated enough to be bold and decisive.

Minor issues became major concerns. Instead of contentedly going through the motions, as I had done for many months, I was now picking fights that I couldn't win, taking stands that I couldn't defend, and instigating battles that did not need to be waged. The once-popular "office Ray" became bi-polar Jekyll and Hyde.

You know, it's hard to be happy at home when you're un-happy at work. My struggle was gradually polluting the home at-mosphere.

Marva would advise me to get out and do something else, anything else. She didn't have the same fears that were holding me back. Yet no matter how strongly she pushed, I couldn't jump, wouldn't jump. I was just too dang-blasted afraid.

Then a pivotal day: I wouldn't/couldn't/didn't jump, so the reinsurance company pushed. I was fired.

Fired. Yikes! For the second time in my life. Double yikes!

Complacency is a subtle enemy. It sneaks up on you. Just when you think that business and life are coming together, the unex-pected comes a'calling and forces its way in.

FINDING YOUR WAY

- Is about finding a path, and sometimes it's about finding an easier path.
- Is still possible even when you've lost your way on another path.
- May begin with finding your way in love, even while losing your way at work.
- Involves balance—balancing the business way and the family way, the career way and the personal way, the way at work and the way at home.
- Will often involve a bumpy ride.

"Be aware of wonder. Live a balanced life —learn some and think some and draw and paint and sing and dance and play and work every day some." — Robert Fulghum

8

FIRED!
NOW
WHAT?

The first time I was fired, I was devastated. This time, I was relieved. The decision to get out had been made for me. The proverbial weight was now lifted from my shoulders.

The question was, "What do I do next?" With Marva's encouragement, and more than a little reassured by the severance check that was part of my termination package, I began to more easily contemplate the concept of returning to self-employment.

The lump sum of six months' pay in combination with Marva's income would surely cover any short-term financial concerns. As a result, with Marva's encouragement, I gave serious thought to finding my way in the world as an entrepreneur.

Finding a way back into self-employment was tough.

Whenever I'd faced tough problems in the past, I'd basically addressed them alone. This time I had help in the form of Marva Zulay Castillo.

She has a direct and simple approach to facing difficult decisions—and for her, career decisions aren't tricky at all: "Do what you love and somehow it will all work out. Find your passion and the income will come."

Naturally, when I'd been thinking of returning to self–employment, my focus had been on going back to selling insurance, perhaps this time as an independent broker. Marva, however, saw more for me. She kept asking me pointed questions: "What would you love to do? What would excite you? Where is your passion?"

As a life insurance agent I had done business with several clients in the photography business. Photography, always a hobby, was now taking on the attraction of a possible business.

Over dinner with a close friend and highly successful businessman, Eric Turner, I mentioned that Marva and I were thinking of getting into something involving photography. His interest was piqued.

"Hey, if you're serious, let me know, maybe we can work something out," he told me.

A short while later, on little more than drive and determination, we opened Raymond's—A Studio of Fine Photography—Preserving Memories of Life's Memorable Moments.

Eric and I became partners and shared equally the cost of equipment, start-up expenses, and the financial costs of getting a new venture up and running.

I spent two intense weeks at the Winona School of Professional Photography just outside Chicago, learning about the creative components of photography as well as the broader issues of running a photography business. Over several weeks, I consulted a multitude of photographers, some who were previously clients, plus others I didn't know, seeking their advice and suggestions on anything and everything that might help our business get off the ground.

We leased space in Yorkville—not far from the auto dealership where I'd worked for three days—the trendiest part of town with its sophisticated art galleries, bistros, antique stores, high-end clothiers, and the most in-vogue bars, clubs, and entertainment hotspots. It was the ideal location for what we thought would be "a boutique studio" that would build a reputation and cater to the upper-end market, those seeking the personal and expensive touch.

Raymond's was a catastrophe from the opening bell. Money disappeared faster than a pizza at a Weight Watchers convention. People who had indicated that they would support us never showed up. A new and innovative "Memories" concept—music-enhanced slide presentations—was received enthusiastically by those who experienced it, while never generating the revenue necessary to cover the increased costs of production.

The severance pay vanished, having been used as seed money.

Next to go was my RRSP (Registered Retirement Savings Plan). Two decades to accumulate; just a few months to disappear.

To survive, Raymond's took on wedding work for other studios.

For a time we covered the rent, phone, and car lease. Still, it wasn't enough to make a profit from which I could take an income.

In the months when we didn't get work from other studios, our fixed expenses significantly exceeded our income. Eric pumped in a few thousand dollars on a regular basis until it became clear that we were going nowhere.

My personal finances were even worse than the studio's. Every month another withdrawal was needed from the RRSP fund. When that ran out, credit cards were pressed into service for cash advances.

Our economic plight was worsened by the fact that Marva had been on maternity leave for six months, having given birth to our son Darien shortly after the studio opened. Although she was back working, the addition to the family meant added childcare costs. Each month we went deeper and deeper into the economic hole.

Finally we had to face the reality of the situation and shut the studio down. We didn't declare bankruptcy; we simply lost all of our money. Nonetheless, I was certainly bankrupt personally, emotionally, spiritually, and intellectually.

It was the bleakest of times.

I'd lost every cent that we had as well as some we didn't.

I was carrying maxed-out, past-due balances on a variety of credit cards.

We sold off the equipment, getting less than forty cents on the dollar, and what we couldn't sell, we gave away or took it home. As I carried the furniture out of the failed enterprise, I began to ask myself "the questions"—the ones we all ask when things don't go the way we expected.

"Why me, Lord?"

"How come my dreams, goals, and aspirations never seem work out?"

"Why can't I ever seem to get the breaks?"

Experts tell us that the brain doesn't judge or interpret. It merely works. When you ask the brain a question, it processes to find an answer and continues to do so until it comes up with one. The brain will find an answer to any request, so be careful what you request.

My internal Mrs. Mackenzie had the answer to all my "why" questions.

"You've got a big mouth, a bad attitude, a chip on your shoulder, and you'll never amount to much!"

FINDING YOUR WAY

- Is based on discovering your passion.
- Involves the strategy of asking for help.
- Means avoiding the tendency to ask disempowering, victim questions
- Requires concentrating instead on asking empowering, inspiring, constructive questions, including:
  - What can I learn from this experience?
  - What's great about this?
  - What could be great about this?
  - How might this help me in the future?
  - Who else is this experience going to help?
  - What terrific lesson is this teaching me?
  - What will I do differently next time?
  - How would I help someone else get through this?

"Only passions, great passions, can elevate the soul to great things."
— Denis Diderot

"The uncreative mind can spot wrong answers, but it takes a very creative mind to spot wrong questions." — Anthony Jay

9

RIGHT
BACK
WHERE
YOU
STARTED
FROM

Following the crash and burn of Raymond's, I was a stay-at-home dad for several months. I told people that I was "weighing my options." In truth, I was doing little more than trying to regain some semblance of self-esteem that had been decimated by the studio's failure.

It quickly became apparent that finding a job, any kind of a job, paying anywhere near the income that I had been making prior to the photography experiment, was highly improbable.

It was a time of serious consolidation in the reinsurance industry and there were many more people on the market than there were positions to be filled. And most of the candidates for these fewer positions had not been away from the business for almost two years, as I had. Also, this world was a small one. My old boss wasn't likely to provide a glowing reference for me.

It was clear that maybe my best option, perhaps my only one, was to go back to selling life insurance. Equally clear, at least in my own head and heart, was the knowledge that starting all over again as an agent scared the daylights out of me.

Fate would once more smile kindly on Alice and Eric's baby boy.

I sought the advice of several people, notably David Ryckman, an ex-colleague from my early days at Canada Life. We had worked closely together during his initial entry into the life insurance business and had developed a friendship that grew stronger over time. I had—and continue to have—enormous respect and admiration for Dave, both as a person and as a businessman, and didn't hesitate to ask for his input.

Dave, like me, had moved on from the good old Canada Life years earlier; unlike me, he had continued to be fully self-employed in the insurance biz. He had established his own brokerage company, building a strong organization and a solid reputation.

As we talked, Dave shared the latest news and scuttlebutt about the insurance business. I found his comments enlightening. I'd lost touch with the sales side of insurance generally—and with the local market specifically—from having spent so much time in the United States.

In return, I was able to tell him what I had learned in the reinsurance arena about how to place the big cases and jumbo applications, a part of the market he was very interested in. The more we chatted, the more both of us came to the same realization: Maybe there was some way we could work together again.

I wanted to get back in the game; Dave needed help. Could there be a win-win here?

My focus was easy to identify: I wanted to get back into selling and knew that I didn't want to start from scratch.

Dave's focus was a wee bit harder for me to make out. It was clear that his client base had grown beyond his ability to service it. I learned that even before our conversation, he had been looking at ways to restructure. On the one hand, he knew that he needed help; on the other hand, he didn't know exactly what kind of help he was looking for. I helped him find it.

Finally the discussion moved to the possibility of my joining forces with Dave, not as an employee, but as an independent associate.

Dave would benefit by improving service to previously ignored clients and having someone in the office to share some of the leadership pressures.

I would benefit by having the chance to jump-start my reentry to personal production. I would gain immediate access to a wide variety of insurance carriers and instant penetration of an accessible market, Dave's existing client base.

I was convinced that I was getting the better part of the deal. Later I learned that Dave felt the same.

The association worked well right from the get-go, especially for me. I had learned from the mistakes that I'd made in the corporate world. I now recognized that internal relationships are as important as client relationships. I paid close attention to establishing strong and respectful interactions with the existing staff. I'd chip in if some grunge work needed to be done. I'd make coffee. I'd bite my tongue when I found myself getting edgy.

With almost unrestricted access to Dave's client database, I was able to generate sales right from the start. Service calls led to review meetings; review meetings resulted in increasing coverage. Call-in leads were forwarded directly to me. I'd go through the files with Dave and he guided me to the clients representing the best opportunities. Business flowed in more easily than I could have ever imagined.

Dave and I engaged in short-term and long-term planning sessions.

He kept me out of potholes that I otherwise might not have seen, and I brought a different perspective to issues that he might have missed.

The Pons/Castillo clan moved out of the city, having bought a terrific house in the suburbs. Marva initiated a career change, also into self-employment, and became an IT consultant with General Electric, resulting in a huge leap in income. She bought herself a red Mazda MX6 sports car. We took regular vacations.

The kids were growing, business was booming, and the next few years were enjoyable, happy, and relaxed.

FINDING YOUR WAY

- Often means getting help from others: those who have traveled the road before you.
- Often means finding counsel—the right counsel.
- Means learning from your mistakes.
- Is easier in times of prosperity.

"Don't follow any advice, no matter how good, until you feel as deeply in your spirit as you think in your mind that the counsel is wise." — David Seabury

"Failure is the foundation of success, and the means by which it is achieved." — Lao Tzu

10

Back onto the Skinny Branches

Sundays are usually a lazy day for the Pons/Castillo family. A day of family chore time followed by family fun time. A day for catching up on all the mundane stuff like laundry, grocery shopping, and gardening. A day that would end maybe with renting a movie or hanging out with neighbors and friends. A day of rest, not work.

One particular Sunday around this time I had the house to myself and was engaged in a serious sports pig-out in front of the TV. It would turn out to be one of those days when the unexpected sneaks up on you.

Patricia was out visiting friends and had taken Darien with her. Marva was in downtown Toronto at a franchise exhibition, after which she was going to take in some of the touristy stuff the big city has to offer.

She had joined the Big Sister organization a few months earlier and had her little sister, Jessica, with her. She had planned nothing more than a little tire-kicking of some business opportunities at the Metro Convention Centre, then a visit to the CN Tower to get tummy tickles from traveling so high in the glass-fronted elevators.

The day would conclude by introducing Jessica to the delicacies of dim sum in one of Marva's favorite restaurants in Chinatown.

The agenda for the day was quickly modified when Marva the franchise show tire-kicker and tourist was converted into Marva the interested franchise purchaser.

Franchising was a phenomenon at the time. It had grown in quantum proportions over the previous decade or so, primarily because it provided a way for wannabe entrepreneurs to go into business for themselves with a safety net. Keen yet hesitant people were able to decrease the risk of opening a business by purchasing a proven system, a turnkey operation.

The group most often credited as the founders of the franchising phenomenon was McDonald's. Their success had been used as the primary example of franchising excellence by business schools, universities, and colleges around the globe.

The cost of a McDonald's, or something similar, had grown to $500,000, $750,000, a million dollars, or more, and was therefore out of reach for most folks, especially first-time entrepreneurs. Enterprising franchisors took note of this. They created more affordable ventures, giving rise to a variety of lower-priced opportunities. People could now open businesses of their own for as little as a few thousand dollars.

Along with this explosion of franchising came the franchise shows, one-stop shopping events for those seeking their once-in-a-lifetime opportunity.

For Marva, this particular show was not so much about finding a business as spending some quality time with Jessica.

For Jessica, the show was a lot more fun than anticipated. She spent her time loading up on the candies, mini chocolate bars, and cookies that were being offered by the exhibitors. She had converted her exhibition bag, intended for brochures and flyers, into a bulging loot bag.

The day ended abruptly, precisely forty-two and a half minutes after the pair rounded Corner Three, Aisle H, between exhibit spaces 89 and 91.

Space 89 was a display for a carpet-cleaning business. This type of franchise held no appeal for Marva, and a lack of goodies made it of no interest to Jessica, who quickly advanced four booths down. Space 91 was a septic tank maintenance service and Marva hardly even noticed it. But space 90 … that was another matter.

"FABUTAN: NORTH AMERICA'S LARGEST INDOOR TANNING COMPANY," announced the eye-catching starburst off to the left of a bright gold banner with the Fabutan company name emblazoned in vibrant scarlet. It stopped Marva in her tracks. Had I been there I would have described her as "gobsmacked," British slang for someone severely taken aback.

For ninety seconds, she remained stunned and stationary. Then she took seven steps forward and advanced herself—and unwitting, unsuspecting me—into the next adventure of our lives.

Marva and I had been indoor tanners for years. I came to the practice the hard way. Our first trip together to her homeland, Venezuela, had been spoiled by my getting severely sunburned before even getting to the beach. I'd sizzled up while on the brief boat ride to one of the islands of Morrocoy, perhaps the most pristine beach reserve in all of South America.

It wasn't entirely my fault. Not really. The swiftly moving launch, which was needed to get from the mainland to the beach, generated a pleasant and cooling breeze and the choppy water cast off plenty of fresh spray, further cooling my body and deceiving my senses.

This process was aided by several well-chilled beers and roncitos that had gone down oh-so-smoothly on the dock while waiting for the lancha to arrive.

(Roncito: fill a glass to the brim with ice, then add rum to halfway up the ice, top off with tonic and add a hefty squeeze of lime.)

By the time I realized I had caught too much sun, it was too late to cover up. I rapidly advanced to pink, and then to bright crimson.

It was three days before I could leave the apartment. Staying indoors was necessary to avoid the sun's rays, of course, but also to avoid looking like a dork in a land of Greek demigods.

I did what I could to circumvent such nonsense the next time I was vacationing: maintain a year-round tan at an electric beach. Twice a week I visited a tanning salon. Occasionally, Marva would tag along and thoroughly tick me off by bronzing in no time flat. I swear that she could get dark sitting in front of a forty-watt incandescent.

The tanning salon that we frequented certainly wasn't the best. However, it was the only game in town. Until space 90 heaved into view, that is.

No one could have imagined the multitude of thoughts ricocheting through Marva's cerebellum during the ninety seconds she stood gobsmacked before the Fabutan booth:

Business ownership made safer through franchising.

Multiple income source, increased diversity, greater security, asset creation.

Tanning—we already use and believe in the product.

Fun—a fun business, not so serious like insurance or computer technology.

Customer service is lousy where we go to tan and yet they're so busy. If they're so busy and the service is crap, then surely we can do well.

Staff will run the place. Managing staff is my specialty. I can do this. Good opportunity to create jobs, help some folks make a few dollars, plus we can help them to grow skills for business and for life.

Ray can sell. He can teach others to sell. I'll manage them, he can teach them, both of us can motivate them. Good combination.

The people manning the booth: They look like nice people, people you can trust.

Biggest tanning company in North America. Big is good. Be the first in Ontario. Get in on the ground floor. Expand as we go. Nothing too tricky: no inventory, no overwhelming investment.

They say the human brain is the world's most powerful computer. Marva had hers going at maximum crank. Then for the following forty minutes she engaged in the first phase of due diligence. She probed and questioned, collected data, and accumulated substantive facts and figures from the Fabutan representatives.

In truth, courtesy of right-brain intuition, right-brain feeling, right-brain gut instinct, she had already decided that this was a venture worthy of pursuing. Now all she needed was enough left-brain logic to not look stupid to other people or herself.

Not more than three, maybe four days earlier, she had been watching a video with Darien, *The Land Before Time*. There is a poignant moment, early in the movie, when a mother dinosaur, with her dying breaths, passes along some last words of advice to her baby dinosaur, Littlefoot: "Let your heart guide you. It whispers, so listen closely."

At that point in the movie, the pause button was immediately engaged, so that Marva the human mother could pass along the same advice to her baby. "Trust your instincts, Darien. Listen to your heart, always. Pay attention to what your whispering intuition is telling you. It will never let you down, but you have to pay attention. Listen well, listen hard, and then have the courage to act according to what you hear."

It was a Kodak moment for Marva; little more than an interruption for Darien.

Now, mere days later, as she was contemplating a decision for herself, standing before space 90, her heart and mind were struggling to come together. Would she have the courage to hear and listen to her own whispering heart?

FINDING YOUR WAY

- Is dancing on the edge, taking a chance, daring to risk.
- Is about trusting your instincts and hearing your inner, whispering voice—which isn't easy to do over the roar of day-to-day life.
- Involves a balance of intuition and analysis: trusting your instincts, but balancing this with logic and reason. Marva's analytical personality, for example, demanded that she get plenty of hard facts when making the decision about the franchise. However, emotionally, her decision had already been made.

"The struggle … to learn to listen to and respect our own intuitive, inner promptings is the greatest challenge of all." — Herb Goldberg

"The best and most beautiful things in the world cannot be seen or even touched. They must be felt with the heart." — Helen Keller

11

EXPECT
THE
UNEXPECTED

All of the above was of course unknown to me on that lazy Sunday afternoon.

I had been watching a little golf, switching occasionally to the NASCAR race, using the ALT/CH button to make switching channels quick and easy. I was on the third of "a coupla beers," while folding the last of four loads of laundry. Me, the remote, Tiger Woods, and the good old boys of NASCAR—could it get any better than this?

I heard her before I saw her. Marva entered the house with a flourish, discarding her usual exuberant "Hola!" in favor of the excited announcement, three times in rapid succession, "I have found our business!"

The smile on her face, the gleam in her eye, and the enthusiasm in her voice were clear evidence that I wasn't going to see any more NASCAR wipeouts.

We talked for hours. Well, she talked, I listened.

Initially, I wasn't nearly as positive as Marva about Fabutan, nor for that matter about expanding into any other business. But neither was I dead set against it.

The longer we talked, the more alluring the possibility of expanding into another business became.

Whenever I said something cautionary or pragmatic, Marva met it with a strong statement of reassurance. Whenever she appeared hesitant, I became the advocate, easily able to list all the reasons for at least going to the next level of investigation.

We switched several times, from champion to detractor, detractor to champion, shuttling from one to the other with ease. The fears of one were soothed by confidence of the other; confidence replaced by doubts; doubts exchanged into belief; belief supplanted by uncertainty.

A seed had been planted, to the point that, within the week, we were willing to invest a few bucks on a trip to Calgary to visit the tanning company's head office. Now both of us were tire-kickers. We wanted to have a look-see at some actual stores, talk to the owners, view the set-up, meet customers, and immerse ourselves fully into the nuts and bolts of the operation. We were tire-kickers with a deposit check in hand and a strong sense of commitment that we would be moving ahead.

We visited four Fabutan outlets. One located near Barlow Trail, close to the airport, and the others closer to the downtown area. A mere two hours after Air Canada flight 843 had touched down at Calgary International Airport, and within minutes of arriving at the head office, we signed the letters of intent, handed over the $5,000 deposit, and became the first Fabutan franchisees east of Alberta.

During the rest of the three-day visit, we worked in a studio, trained in the system, and were bombarded with an overwhelming amount of information to prepare us to open our own store. Busy though we were, we also found time to whoop it up a bit at night.

On the journey home, we were exhausted, exhilarated, and raring to go, eager to find the perfect spot for our new escapade.

The very next day a business loan was approved and in place for $75,000. The franchise fee would gobble up $25,000, and $50,000, was needed for equipment, supplies, and operating funds. It would be tight, but it was doable.

"Never amount to much, Mrs. Mackenzie? Well perhaps a credit rating that allowed for an almost instant loan approval of seventy-five thousand smackers might suggest otherwise."

The next day we hunted for a location. One spot got our immediate attention: eleven hundred square feet of bare space in a brand new strip plaza that already had high traffic volume because of the huge supermarket across the parking lot and a Wal-Mart located right next door. An ideal location. Three days after first viewing this "prime commercial property," we signed a five-year lease.

Within ten hectic days, and after a multitude of 1–800 calls to the Alberta head office for guidance, designs for the studio were confirmed, plans were finalized, and construction began.

And the day the work began, we left for a two-week, all-inclusive vacation at a spiffy new resort in the Dominican Republic. Now there's timing for you. The walls are going up in a brand new business venture, and Marva, Ray, and the kids were headed off for two weeks of fun in the sun.

The vacation didn't make complete sense to me. Then again, it had been planned, and paid for, for weeks. What else were we to do? I wasn't about to forfeit the total cost of the trip, and I didn't relish the idea of staying home alone while the family frolicked without me. So I decided we'd all go. I'd eat too much, drink too much, relax, and recharge. Hey, at least I'd get myself an ideal tan for the opening of this brand spanking new tanning enterprise.

FINDING YOUR WAY

- Sometimes means trusting the one you love.
- Requires dealing with change.
- Sometimes means taking an action that doesn't make complete sense and having enough faith that things will somehow work out.

"All life is a chance. The [person] who goes furthest is the one who is willing to do and dare." — Dale Carnegie

12

SETTING RECORDS

Returning from two weeks in the Caribbean, I looked very much like the owner of a tanning business, and Marva even more so. Now it was time to roll up our sleeves, put the finishing touches to the studio, and watch the business reality match the business visualized.

It was anticipated that the store would open about one week after our return. Yeah, right.

There are so many things to take care of when opening a new enterprise, and although we had indeed planned for the "expected unexpected," we had woefully underestimated. We had been self–employed, between the two of us, for almost two decades. But, and it's a big but, opening this retail operation clearly demonstrated that starting a one-man-band personal-service operation was very different from starting a retail store.

Most noticeably, we were dealing with many more people than merely ourselves. Coordinating their different levels of motivation, effort, and sense of urgency was proving a lot more challenging than anticipated. The cast included electricians, plumbers, carpenters, advertising people, leasing agents, lawyers, printers, more advertising people, carpet installers, municipal inspectors, tax officials, bureaucrats, delivery people, and yet more advertising people.

A multitude of other issues also needed to be handled. Tanning beds were ordered and scheduled for delivery, only to be held hostage in customs for almost two weeks because of an over-zealous customs agent who believed that the cross-border transaction called for import duties and taxes of a whopping $9,000. The tax turned out not to be required; it was, nonetheless, a harrowing time.

Interviewing potential staff was especially difficult. Neither Marva nor I had much of an idea about the type of employee we were looking for.

Compliance with all of the building code regulations slowed some construction issues down to the speed of a snail on valium.

Finally, somehow, inexplicably, it all got done. Our shiny new store opened for business one day shy of four weeks late.

Opening day was a Tuesday. I was standing behind the counter, eager to serve the customers. Marva sat in one of the chairs in the modest waiting area. Each of us had a mile-wide smile and an unbridled eagerness to knock the socks off any customer willing to give us a try. And knock their socks off we did—all six of them!

In a twelve-hour day, six people entered the place, seven if you counted the window cleaner, whose only reason for coming in was to ask if we wanted the front window cleaned for five bucks a week. I said yes, so the net profit for opening day was a loss of five dollars.

Day one didn't fill us, the proud owners, with much confidence.

By closing time, the beaming smiles were long gone. In the evening, over a glass of Merlot, we rationalized that the flyers announcing the studio opening had not yet gone out, so we shouldn't rush to judgment about results. Marva made a statement in the form of a question: "Tomorrow will be good, right babe?" I hoped that my immediate and enthusiastic "You betcha" masked the concerns I was feeling.

Day two was very similar. This time, nine people came in. The late-night rationalizing was less enthusiastic.

Day three experienced a boost to all of nineteen customers, three of whom were returning customers from day one. This increase all by itself may have been enough for a more optimistic late-night discussion, because after all, when tension is high, even the most minor of improvements can stimulate hope. But an added and more valid reason for increased enthusiasm was nestled in the local newspaper waiting for us on our driveway, proclaiming: "ONE WEEK UNLIMITED FREE TANNING." The flyers had begun distribution.

The marketing strategy that had proven so successful for other Fabutan stores was to bombard the area with flyers for one week of free tanning. The Fabutan starburst logo that had gobsmacked Marva at the franchise show was used as the design for the promotional flyers, and these mini logos proved as eye-catching in this smaller format as the franchise show version had been.

Five thousand flyers a week would be sent out for four to six weeks after opening. The idea was to generate traffic, stimulate interest, and provide exposure for the new store. I had wondered how this would result in real revenue and legitimate paying customers. Nevertheless, I was willing to suppress doubts and follow the system.

Follow the system.

I was reminded of when I had first joined the life insurance business, all those years back, and the challenge of Tony Lawes when interviewing me, as well as on the first days of training:

"We will tell you how to be successful. It is up to you to decide whether you will do it."

For me, buying the franchise was in many ways the same thing.

Fabutan had a record of success, a system, established from the previous sixty-five successful openings. Follow the system. It's been proven before, many times over. Work the system and there is every reason to believe that the system will work for you.

The flyer that I now held in my hand was evidence of the system at work. Many people just like us were probably gazing at the announcement of this new retailing marvel.

As I drifted off to sleep that night, I wondered what the following day would bring.

The phone was ringing even before we got the store open, and the darned thing didn't stop ringing for the rest of the day.

I'd calculated that for a five-bed studio offering appointments every half-hour, the maximum number of clients per day was 120. Simple math: 10 (clients per hour) x 12 (hours per day) = 120 (maximum clients per day). On this day, the number of clients served was 165! It was a hectic, frantic, exhilarating, exhausting time. It was the most exciting day four that we ever could have imagined.

At 9:35 p.m., thirty-five minutes past the expected close, the last customers had left and we locked the doors. We had gone from gruesome to awesome in less than seventy-two hours.

Marva let out a subdued, restrained, almost whispered, and soul-inspiring "Yyyyesssss!"

Then she hugged me with a passionate, powerful embrace, kissed me full on the lips, pulled back, looked into my eyes, and said: "Baby ... you stink."

We laughed like giddy children.

She was right of course. I'd been running around all day, sanitizing and cleaning the beds, and sweat was rolling off me like I was still on the beaches of Morrocoy. I was as pungent as a rich Camembert. It was the greatest compliment she could have given me.

We set about tackling the mountain of paperwork, client cards, and administrative items that we had been forced to put to one side. Then I got to deal with the money.

Money? Revenue? Oh yes, even though every customer was a freebie for tanning, there were a multitude of small sales for peepers, the mandatory eye protection that other tanning places provided for free. Fabutan insisted that every customer buy their own personal eye wear ("Do you really want to use germ-infested eyewear that a multitude of other people have worn and handled?") and this alone generated a few hundred dollars in sales. Toss in several sales of lotions, tanning accelerators, and creams, and the day's take was a little more than seven hundred bucks.

Doubts that had been prompted by the dismal results of the first three days were replaced by euphoria of day four success.

The next several days showed no let-up.

At most tanning salons, customer service consisted of little more than an abrupt instruction of where to go: "Room 3, twenty minutes." At a Fabutan studio—trumpet fanfare: "North America's Largest Indoor Tanning Company"—it was mandated that each new client receive a detailed explanation of how and why a tan was achieved and how to get the most out of their Fabutan experience. Each client was then personally introduced to the tanning equipment and given instructions on how to turn on the equipment, operate the fan, and adjust the sound system.

The procedure did take time. It also got a lot of nice comments from clients, both from people who had never been in a tanning bed before and from experienced veterans who had been tanning indoors for years. No matter how tempted we were to abbreviate the process, especially when we got really busy, with customers lined up four deep at the counter, we patiently followed the system. After a while, we had it pretty well under control.

After two furiously satisfying weeks, Marva returned to her IT consulting work, leaving me to look after the studio with Kate, our newly acquired studio manager, who had been hired by Marva a few days earlier. Kate was a perky blonde with an hourglass figure, bubbly personality, and infectious energy. She was filled to over-flowing with all the charm and charisma of the commonly de-scribed, yet uncommonly encountered, girl next door.

A week later it was time for me to leave the studio in Kate's hands and go back to my insurance practice. This I did, while con-tinuing to maintain daily contact with the new enterprise.

Each morning I would go in for a pre-opening tan, and then engage in a quick or lengthy chat with Kate to see how things were going. Throughout the day I'd make plenty of calls, usually for no other reason than to check in. I was ready at a moment's notice to drop whatever insurance case I might be working on to deal with any studio issue that needed my personal attention. If the studio was busy enough to warrant an extra hand to look after the now paying clients, Kate knew that I could be there to help out. The insurance practice was my business; the studio was my baby.

In the ninth week, I heard some exciting news from the Cal-gary head office. I knew that business was pretty good from the daily bank deposits and the daily updates of QuickBooks that I was using to keep track of the financial metrics. What I did not know, and the reason for the call being made, was that the studio had set a record. I was congratulated with the words:

"You have done the most business ever, in the first six weeks of opening, by any new franchise, anywhere, including new studios right here in Calgary, the tanning capital of the world."

My baby was making me proud.

Now it should be said that some of that record-setting success was attributable to the fact that, with the cost of living in the Greater Toronto Area being higher than in Western Canada, we had been given approval to up our prices.

Whatever the reason, it was cause for celebration.

Instead of calling Marva immediately with the good news, I ordered the seventy-five-piece sushi/sashimi combo from our favorite Japanese restaurant, the aptly named Sush Sushi, and laid out a surprise picnic in the family room. I then prepared a martini for me and a bubble bath for her, leaving another batch of martinis brewing in the refrigerator.

An hour or so later, the now successful business partners celebrated their success. The exotic and exquisite food was devoured slowly, almost sensually, and was washed down with liberal quantities of hot sake kept warm in, of all things, our Mr. Coffee coffeemaker. A lovely evening.

I tingled on the skin, thanks to a rare afternoon tan taken two hours earlier. I tingled in the tummy from the martinis and sake. And I tingled all over from the satisfaction of the sales record that had been set, and a sense that maybe, just maybe, we were going to realize the triumph that Marva had envisioned several months back.

Ironically, the very next day was a day of zero revenue, the first since day three, which dated back more than eight weeks.

It was not the last.

Business dropped off severely. In fact, it plummeted. Even when people did show up, it was usually to spend tanning minutes they had already purchased, not to buy more.

The studio set yet another record in the following six months: the least amount of business in the history of the chain.

For the next six months, expenses far exceeded revenue. We were doing even less business than a studio located in a village of only fifteen thousand people. Kate did everything she could to encourage sales, but to no avail. "This is the last of your sessions—would you like to buy another package?" She batted her eyelids if it was a male client, and gave a big smile to the females. Only to receive, all too often, the response, "No thanks. Not right now—but I'll be back in the fall. See you then."

The euphoria of the sushi night was replaced by the reality of our financial situation. Gleeful optimism turned into business-owner blues. Hope and potential became sadness and concern. The martinis of celebration became the martinis of drown your sorrows. Our quantum leap had turned into a quantum leap off a cliff. Again.

A wise person once commented that whatever doesn't kill you will make you stronger. I sure as hell didn't feel that I was being made any stronger. I could put on a good front for the staff. I'd have optimistic things to say for the kids and family. Once in a while I'd even have positive things to say to myself.

However, all of the positive affirmations didn't speak nearly as loudly as the negative tapes embedded in my brain.

Mrs. Mackenzie was front and center yet again, yelling, "Pons, you'll never amount to much—never!"

Toss in a plethora of my own pessimistic self-talk:

"Who do you think you are?"

"Are you nuts?"

"How dare you do this to me?"

Next, add the gloomy headlines in newspapers and magazines about a general economic downturn in business, a "natural and needed adjustment."

Then try to say, "Let your heart guide you. It whispers, so listen closely."

Sometimes if you listen to your heart, you could lose your sanity. I came close.

FINDING YOUR WAY

- Is never easy.
- Demands facing the reality of results.
- Sometimes means not listening.

"Many [people] owe the grandeur of their lives to their tremendous difficulties." — Charles Haddon Spurgeon

13

THE
REWARDS
WILL
COME

Every successful business owner, without exception, goes through tough times. In the grand scheme of things, compared with the trials and tribulations of other owners and entrepreneurs, what I was experiencing wasn't that terrible. Nonetheless, for me it was incapacitating and debilitating.

I was learning the difference between an economic recession and depression. You may have heard it before. A recession is when your neighbor is out of work. A depression is when you are.

I crunched the numbers. The monthly overhead was $9,000 a month. We would have some guaranteed income of about $3,200 a month from clients with automatic debits for unlimited tanning memberships, leaving a monthly shortfall of around $5,800.

The studio was open three hundred hours a month. Just twenty bucks an hour and we would at least break even. Two hundred bucks a day. Shouldn't be that hard, should it? After all, only a couple of weeks earlier, we were regularly doing a thousand a day.

Zero days were frequent. Some of the unlimited tanning clients put a hold on their memberships. The automatic debits dipped from $3,200 a month to $1,200. Revenue fell short of overhead by $4,000, $5,000, $6,000 a month. One tough week followed another. And yet another.

It's been said that the tough times will make you or break you. Baloney! The tough times don't make you or break you ... they reveal you. These times, and how you deal with them, ultimately determine whether success will be yours. Character counts!

My hope was at its lowest. My core values were being put to the test. How was I to be revealed?

After three months of dismal revenue, the business bank account was insufficient to cover payroll. What was I to do? After several hours of finagling with the bookkeeping software, crunching the business account numbers, crunching the personal account numbers, the only solution I could come up with was to use a personal credit card to transfer funds into the business account.

Borrow from Peter in order to pay Paul, and do it at 18.75 percent interest.

Thank goodness for the invention of ATMs. This kind of transaction was best done via the anonymity of one of these electronic tellers. I didn't want to conduct the funds transfer with a real live human one. That would be to advertise our economic woes and make it even harder for us to attract business. Using the ATM was my business-owner, intellectual, strategic decision.

The truth was that I didn't want to ask for the transfer from a living, breathing person because I wanted to avoid embarrassment.

The sunshine of a perfect summer day wasn't able to elevate my bleak mood as I walked to the bank. As I entered the vestibule that housed the ATMs, I was feeling more and more dejected. The place was empty. Good. No one will witness my low finance.

I stepped up to the first machine and what did I see? Pay dirt! Nestled in the cash withdrawal tray were five crisp twenty-dollar bills. A hundred bucks, tax free, found money, oh boy!

My first reaction was to grab the money and run. My mind processed a multitude of reasons in the space of only a few seconds in order to justify this action:

Banks are making billions—I mean billions—in profits every year.

A hundred bucks; they won't miss it; it won't make a dent in their massive returns.

Who's gonna know? Nobody's here; there's no way I can get caught.

I can pick up dinner and a bottle of wine, and have enough to treat the kids to a night at the movies.

We deserve a little good luck.

During this internal monologue I secreted the cash into the right-hand pocket of my sweatpants and headed outside. Not three steps toward the parking lot, however, I recognized that no matter how I tried to justify it, keeping the money was stealing. I was being revealed to be a thief. I was being revealed to be weak-willed. I was being revealed to be a man of selective integrity, all too ready to abandon my beliefs for a lousy hundred bucks.

Feeling sheepish, I did a U-turn and re-entered the bank, this time going through the ATM lobby and into the branch.

"Personal Banker – Account Manager" was the title on the badge of the first bank representative I met.

"This was sticking out of machine number one."

"That's not possible."

"Excuse me?"

"It's not possible. Those machines are checked daily. They are completely reliable. You must be mistaken."

Maybe I would get to keep the cash after all. I pressed on: "Well the ATM closest to the window had these bills sticking out of it."

"It can't be."

"But, it did."

"Are you sure?"

"What? What do you mean am I sure?"

My perplexed amusement was turning into indignant frustration.

"I tell you what, how be I just keep the cash?"

"Oh, well … I suppose if you put it like that."

Five minutes later, I left the bank, having convinced the account manager that the money belonged to them, not me. At her insistence I gave her my name and address. Then I returned to the ATM to fulfill my original plan.

On the walk home, I had a little more bounce in my step. The harshness of my financial condition somehow seemed not quite so overbearing.

Not more than four hours later, I was to fully appreciate just how important this moment was for me, as a person and a parent.

At 5:15 p.m. the doorbell rang. My boy, Darien, answered, expecting it to be a buddy collecting him for a game of street hockey, a regular event on summer evenings.

"Poppa, it's for you," he yelled, at a decibel level a town crier would envy.

"Who is it, son?"

"I dunno."

My suspicion was that it would be Jehovah's Witnesses, door-to-door marketing, or some other nuisance interruption to be quickly dispensed with.

"Hello, how can I help you?"

"Are you Mr. Pons?"

Okay here we go, sales pitch, wonder what for?

"Yes. How can I help you?"

"My name's Robert, Bob, Bob Carter. It was my hundred dollars that you returned at the CIBC earlier today, and I wanted to come by and well … uh … thank you for your honesty and … to uh, well, to say thank you in person."

I couldn't think of anything to say.

"It's been a tough go of things for me recently, Mr. Pons, and well, I, uh, I don't think you could know how much this, uh, means to me. Thank you. I mean it, thank you."

The man was barely able to control his emotions. Boy could I relate to that.

"Here's a little something to express my appreciation."

He pushed a gift-wrapped package from Laura Secord toward me, shook my hand with several forceful pumps, and looked ready to say something else. Instead, he just muttered another heartfelt thank you, turned on his heel, and beat a relieved retreat.

It was only a brief exchange: thirty or forty-five seconds, one minute at most. I will remember it forever.

"Who was that, Poppa? Hey what's that? He gave you a present? Cool. Why'd he give you a present, Poppa? What is it? Can we open it? Can we?"

I told my son the tale of finding the hundred bucks and giving it back, and how this gift was from the man whose money I had returned. Then we opened the gift and enjoyed the yummy chocolates. I told the tale a second time an hour later when Marva, now known as Queen Bee, came home. That night I went to bed feeling happier than I had felt in a while, maybe even a little smug.

The following day, right in the midst of the darkest period for the studio, we had a revenue day that was reminiscent of the heyday period. An out-of-the-blue $600 day. Cool.

Then I got a call from an insurance client. "Ray, my accountant tells me that I need to buy another million. Can you swing by later this week and put the paperwork together?"

Without doing a thing, a bunch of business had fallen into my lap. It must be a coincidence, right? No way!

You always get paid for what you do—but not always when you do it.

This time the reward did find me right away.

FINDING YOUR WAY

- Is often more about finding a way, any way, through the tough times.
- Can be expensive.
- Is about doing the right thing—always. Character is not about how you conduct yourself when people are watching, it's about what you do when no one is watching. What decisions do you make when you could get off scot-free? Who are you at your core, when it is possible not to be found out?
- Is about doing the right thing without expecting that good fortune will follow. It's about doing the right thing knowing that good fortune will follow … eventually.

"Life's challenges are not supposed to paralyze you, they're supposed to help you discover who you are." — Bernice Johnson Reagon

14

A
SLOW
RECOVERY

After my ATM heroics, the studio didn't suddenly start generating large profits, but at least we had stopped the heavy bleeding.

Over the next few weeks and months, the debt load remained at a fairly constant level. We were still in a hole, but it wasn't getting any deeper. Many weeks were slightly better than break-even. Times were still tough, but there was a speck of light at the end of the tunnel, and, it no longer appeared to be a train heading right at me.

The line of credit had been extended to the limit. Any deeper and it would have sunk the business. Not for the first time I had been contemplating whether to shut the studio down, to avoid throwing good money after bad. In fact, the thought of closure was an almost daily affair. I recalled the failure of the photography studio, and I most vividly remembered my decisiveness to shut her down and accept the loss. The Fabutan Studio seemed an eerily similar experience. I was leaning toward pulling the plug.

Make the call, Ray; it's time to give up.

Thankfully I didn't make that call. Encouraged by even the

slightest upturn of business, I somehow found the resolve to keep going.

In October, we actually made a tiny profit. With the arrival of the cold weather, the previous clients returned, true to their promises in the spring. Some even brought new clients with them. The busy time revived our flagging spirits and we entered the New Year with renewed determination.

In our inaugural year, we enjoyed only a few weeks of the peak period for tanning, even though our opening advertising blitz extended it a couple of weeks more than usual. This New Year allowed us to make good on the entire tanning season.

The busy season ran for five solid months, and we were able to attract many more of the year-round tanning members, which boosted the pre-authorized deposits on the first of every month to a most healthy level. With fully fifty to sixty percent of the monthly overhead covered on the very first day of the month, we were able to build a financial cushion during the busy months that would more than hold us through the quieter period.

For the next four years the studio turned a reasonable profit.

Our original intent had been to get one studio up and running and then quickly open several others, maybe as many as eight or more. The plan was to take advantage of Marva's exemplary people–management skills by having her run the Fabutan network. If this meant she had to leave the world of IT, well that would be just fine. She had been finding the world of computers rewarding, financially, but stressful, personally. A move into running a retail chain could be a wonderful switch.

After a few years of owning the store, her original plan was no longer quite so enticing to her. Her skill set in dealing with minimum-wage part-timers was less effective than when managing a group of highly paid, independent computer technicians. Now she was refocused on other bigger-picture options.

As for me, I was relieved to be mostly free of the strains of the first year, yet I was no longer feeling the initial excitement for my baby. The studio had become a nice sideline. It was also a nice *distracting* sideline.

I had developed a habit of spending far too much time away from my insurance practice. I was continuing to dedicate many hours to looking after the baby, even though the baby no longer needed me. I had become a prisoner of the very business that was supposed to set me free. I could find ways to fritter away whole days taking care of minor problems that should have been handled by staff.

I felt that something had to be done, and the reality of this was revealed to me after a two-week vacation. On my first day back, I discovered that our newly hired manager had embezzled almost the entirety of the cash sales. More than two grand, and she had the nerve to think that I'd be dumb enough not to notice.

After many in-depth discussions, and with heavy hearts, we made the decision to sell. I mean, this was my baby, the baby that almost died. This was the struggling venture that was rescued, re-suscitated and brought back from the brink of failure. It was indeed with heavy hearts that we decided to sell.

Our heavy hearts were made lighter when, by taking advantage of tax laws that allow for the sale of small businesses as a tax-advantaged capital gain, we sold it for a cool profit of $100,000, tax-free!

FINDING YOUR WAY

- Requires persistence, determination, and doggedness.
- Demands focus, using your highest-value talents, and avoiding low-value "busy" distractions.
- Will occasionally bring windfall rewards.

"Never give in, never give in, never, never, never, never—in nothing, great or small, large or petty—never give in except to convictions of honour and good sense. Never yield to force; never yield to the apparently overwhelming might of the enemy." — Winston Churchill

15

FINDING
MY
VOICE

We settled back into the routine of daily life, but for me, something was missing. Initially I put my ennui down to the natural adjustment after selling off the business. But I knew that wasn't the cause when the feeling persisted long after the sale.

Over the course of time, the lethargy evolved into downright discomfort and I sought out the help of my mastermind group.

Masterminding is the concept of gathering at regular intervals with like-minded individuals to help one another accomplish more.

Once a month my group would get together for an early breakfast and share ideas, exchange suggestions, and attempt to resolve the problems or worries we were going through.

Each person in this group was an active member of Toastmasters International, an organization that helps people become better communicators and overcome their fear of public speaking. We were all members of the Towns of York club in Aurora, and one of the troupe, Ross Mackay, had a few years earlier placed third in the World Championship of Public Speaking—third-best speaker in the entire world. Yikes! For several years he had been a full-time professional speaker and yet maintained his membership with the "amateurs" of Towns of York to continue refining his skills.

Over the years, inspired by Ross's example, and encouraged by the group, I had also participated in speech competitions. Twice I competed at the regional finals, the last leg before the world championship. On both occasions I placed second to the person who went on to place second in the world championship. Close but no cigar.

Inner voice: "Second, to the person who finished second to the world champion, hmm, I must be quite good wouldn't you say?"

I began to wonder what it would be like to become a professional speaker, just like Ross.

But then Mrs. Mackenzie's voice would once more hold me back. I mean, it's one thing to do okay in competitions, quite another to make a living at it. Audiences at competition venues love and admire you for simply giving it a try. It's quite another thing to imagine that people will want you to speak and actually pay you for doing it.

The negative messages in my brain resurfaced.

Why would anyone want to listen to you speak?

What makes you so special, hotshot?

Who do you think you are? You'll never amount to much.

Yeah, right, get real.

Furthermore, I was making a very good living from my insurance practice. It's not bragging if it's the truth. For me it was hard to walk away from the big income to pursue a dream. Money was holding me back from truly embracing the possibility of a career as a speaker. And while it might be true to say that money isn't everything, it does rank right up there with oxygen.

The good income; the negative messages running in my head; the crash and burn of Raymond's; the near crash and burn of Fabutan; the check for forty-seven cents; the present ease of current finances—all of it was keeping me where I was, rather than giving me the courage to go where I wanted to be.

But the seed of my becoming a speaker had been planted. Mistakes of the past were noted, pragmatic concerns recognized, and inadequacies acknowledged. However, the desire for a better future was not to be denied.

It took a good year before I gained even marginal clarity on how to give the idea substance. Bringing a "systems" approach to my problem, I had for some time been doodling with the money targets. I crunched the numbers: Desired income, say, $100,000. That's fifty audiences paying $2,000 a pop. Possible? No way! I mean two grand, fifty times a year, that's like what, one a week? Is that doable? Not a chance!

Okay, perhaps a hundred audiences at $1,000, what about that? No way! How the heck am I going to get someone to pay me a thousand dollars, twice a week?

Well, what about $500? Can you get someone to pay you five hundred, Ray, just five hundred bucks? Maybe. That fee should be acceptable, but where on earth do I find two hundred of them?

And all of this without my ever having been paid, not even once, to make any speech or presentation. If I couldn't get the most realistic of the doodling to make sense, how was I ever going to make the real numbers do so?

During this time, when listening to an audio program of Brian Tracy, I was struck by the segment where he mentioned the notion that figuring out how to get one biggie deal is sometimes easier than trying to get a multitude of little deals. Intrigued, I began contemplating how I might find one big opportunity to become a well-paid speaker. Maybe there was one sponsor that would provide the income figure that I wanted and give me the chance to speak on a regular basis. How might I find such a chance? Danged if I knew!

A few days after that contemplation and a few months after selling the studio, I shared my confused thoughts during the mastermind meeting. Anne Fung, the financial planner of the group, immediately announced, "I've got exactly what you need!"

"Huh?"

"We've been looking to hire someone for ages to train our financial planners in areas of insurance and estate planning; to put on training sessions. It never occurred to me that you'd be interested. Do you want me to set up a meeting?"

Within a few days, meetings had been held, my résumé perused, and I was hired as insurance specialist by one of Canada's largest financial-planning firms. The salary was about thirty percent lower than my hoped-for income, but an incentive bonus would narrow the gap.

In any event, my plan was to be there for only a short time, a year, maybe a year and a half, as a stepping stone to becoming a genuine professional speaker.

I knew I could do all right in competitions. This trainer position seemed the perfect way for me to see if I could make it in the tougher world of business speaking. Four, five, six times a week I'd have the chance to speak, make presentations, provide training sessions, and go from competitive toastmaster to perhaps competent professional.

It was brilliant. I couldn't have been more excited, energized, and keyed up. I was responsible for four offices and would conduct formal training sessions as well as providing one-to-one coaching and consulting. PowerPoint presentations became part of my day-to-day routine, and I quickly gained a reputation for putting on sessions that were enjoyable and fun and, perhaps most importantly, that drew business to the company and the financial planner. My first year showed massive increases in policies sold and premium volume.

I was reminded of Marva's assertion all those years ago: "Do what you love and somehow it will all work out. Find your passion and the income will come. Find your passion!"

Speaking seemed to be my passion. Each day I was eager to get to work, eager to make progress, eager to pursue my passion.

In just a matter of seven or eight months, the passion culminated in a regional conference that I arranged for all four offices, held at a fabulous resort in beautiful Muskoka. It was a day-long event that involved several speakers on a variety of training topics. I was the host of the event as well as one of the keynote presenters.

The day was a huge success. Each presentation was informative and enjoyable. They learned, they laughed, they left a little bit richer than when they came in: richer in knowledge, in understanding, and in wisdom. Three or four hundred people had experienced a valuable day.

Some said the conference was every bit as good as the national conventions attended not by three or four hundred but by two or three thousand. Great things are possible when you follow your passion.

As long as the passion remains strong.

FINDING YOUR WAY

- Means joining a good group—hanging around with the right crowd.
- Involves having an idea and then having either the patience to wait for its time to come or the determination to force its time to be now.
- Is about pursuing your passion.

"There is nothing more powerful than an idea whose time has come." — Victor Hugo

16

❦

QUEEN
BEE
SPEAKS

Having experienced the euphoric high of speaking to this larger group, the prospect of going back to addressing groups of four or five, maybe ten or twelve, was, well, underwhelming.

Many of the folks who came to the local office sessions were there as prisoners—forced to attend on the instruction of their manager. And as professional licensing requirements became more stringent, the prisoner quotient at each event crept ever higher.

Prisoners are rarely reluctant to let their status be known. As a result, more and more time during training sessions was spent moaning, whining, and complaining and less time spent on learning. Common utterances were Buts and Yabuts. And when these prisoners would "but" in, I butted right back.

When I was first hired, I hardly noticed the prisoners. But as complacency set in, I saw them all too clearly.

It wasn't long before my complacency turned into hostility, hostility extended to discomfort, and discomfort inevitably advanced to misery.

Misery is not something that I'd done well with in the past, and this situation was to prove no different. Misery, while multifaceted in nature, is often dealt with in a single-faceted manner.

Am I the only person who has ever needed to learn the same lesson more than once? Am I the only one who has had to re-record over my internal recordings, to reprogram my mindset over and over and over again? I don't suppose that I am.

First I engaged in going through the motions, and before long, as I'd done at the reinsurance company, I was once again instigating battles that didn't need to be waged. One more time I quit and stayed. Like some kind of prison warden, the paycheck kept me in the position that was causing the misery.

Marva had said nothing when I was content and untroubled. Now that I was miserable, that would change—big time!

Back when I was going through the motions at the reinsurance company, she had put up with my shenanigans and bided her time before finally passing comment. This time she tolerated my nonsense for mere weeks.

I received a phone call from her while I was working at the office located just a two-minute walk from our home. I thought she was at the Mississauga office of her current IT contract.

"Hi babe, I'm home," she said. "Can you get away for a few minutes? I want to talk to you."

"I've got a meeting in about an hour, honey. Can it wait?"

"It won't take long. You'll be back in no time."

Marva met me the moment I walked in the door.

"What's the matter with you?" she said.

"What?"

"What's the matter with you?"

"Narrow it down a little for me, babe," I said.

"Okay, pay attention! Why are you doing what you are doing? You're miserable. You're making the kids miserable. You're making me miserable. You'd better do something about it. Do something and do something soon, if you ever again expect to have sex!"

Now she had my full and undivided attention. "What are you talking about?" I said, trying hard not to sound whiny.

"Why are you still doing what you're doing? It's not your passion. You're a great speaker and what you're doing now doesn't let your passion show. It's all right, but it's not your passion. You can do better than this. Now explain to me what's going on!"

"Now wait a minute, babe," I said, thinking fast. "I may not be doing what I really want to do, I may not be following my passion, but hey let's get real here, okay? I'm not doing what I would truly love to be doing, but it does put a roof over our head, keep the wolf from the door, and put food on the table."

Ha! Ray 1, Queen Bee 0.

Queen Bee flew to the kitchen junk drawer. After some rummaging around, she was back with a small notepad and pen.

"Say that again," she said.

"What?"

"Say that again."

"Why?"

"So I can write it down."

"Why?"

"So that when you die, I can inscribe it on your tombstone: 'Here lies Ray Pons. He would have been a great speaker but never gave it a try because he was too busy, putting a roof over our head, keeping the wolf from the door, and putting food on the table.' "

Don't you hate it when they're right? Married people reading this know what I mean.

We spoke for only a few minutes more and then Queen Bee returned to work and I went off to my meeting. I might as well have been somewhere else. My thoughts were on Marva's exhortations. My attention was certainly not on whether we should have Maxwell House or Nabob coffee in the office kitchen.

Timidity must be genetic. I must have been biologically destined to be a Nervous Norman, deficient in daring. How else to explain the struggle that I was having when trying to summon up the guts to leave a job that I hated? No matter how much support I had from Queen Bee, I continued to hold back from making a move.

I kept going through the motions. Turning up, putting in time without putting in meaning, only rarely trying my best. Weeks became months; months became quarters; quarters became three years. Until … You know what's coming, right?

Friday, March 9, 2001, I got a call from my boss: "Ray, will you be in your office Monday?"

"I was planning to be in Owen Sound, Darlene. Why do you ask?"

"I'm coming in to see you. Maybe you could change your plans. See you Monday around ten."

Her tone was pleasant and congenial.

After hanging up, I called Queen Bee. "Hey babe, guess what? Monday I'm getting fired."

"Yeah, right."

"I'm serious. Darlene just called and she didn't say it but I know that Monday I'll be done."

"Sweetheart, I wouldn't be unhappy if that did happen, but I'm telling you they can't give you Insurance Specialist of the Year six months ago and fire you on Monday. It must be something else. Maybe they want to promote you to head office."

"You'll see."

I took off for home, cracked open a beer, and began the weekend early. On Monday morning I went into the office early and started packing up my stuff. It was eerie to know exactly what was coming. At 10:30 or so, apologizing for being late, Darlene arrived and we walked back to my office. Never known for being passive when dealing with issues large or small, Darlene got straight to the point.

"Ray, you have a great future ahead of you—but it's not with us."

"I know, Darlene."

"What?"

"I told Marva right after you called that you were coming to fire me. She disagreed. I knew."

"Wow, well, listen Ray, there's a consultant here with me who's supposed to help you with your transition. He's waiting in the reception area. Shall I send him in?"

"No, I'm good. Why don't I just sign the papers that I'm sure you must have and then we can both of us get outta here."

It wasn't that I was trying to be cavalier with Darlene. It was simply that I'd become tired of pretending and playing games. It was time to get it done and move on to whatever was next. In minutes I was off to the next adventure. Reality check noted, learning considered, next stop contemplated.

FINDING YOUR WAY

- Demands being able to deal with difficult people.
- Is realizing that a strategy that didn't work in the past is unlikely to be a sound strategy in the present.
- Is about facing reality and moving on.

"It is too difficult to think nobly when one thinks only of earning a living." — Jean-Jacques Rousseau

"The man who does not work for the love of work but only for money is not likely to make money nor find much fun in life." — Charles M. Schwab

17

Is
Now
the
Time?

Strike three! Or, as a baseball umpire might say, "STEEERIKE THREEEEEE!"

Four jobs had—one time quit, three times fired.

After a while, even those of us in the slow group finally learn the lessons life keeps teaching us. The lesson for me was that I'm a great team player—as long as I own the team.

Having a good job within a good company gives many people a sense of security. For me, it brings frustration.

Like it or not, there's something in my DNA that says self-employment is my only truly viable career option. I'm never going to get the gold watch for length of service.

Having been released from what I realized to be the bond-age—however well paid—of employment, I did feel liberated. I'd been set free to clarify, pursue, and attain my passion. I felt confident that maybe, just maybe, I was ready to be fully engaged in finding my way.

The feeling proved justified. Finding my way at this phase in my life wasn't nearly as difficult as searches in years gone by.

My heart, my softly speaking inner voice, was telling me that my passion was public speaking. Would I have the ears to hear it and the courage to trust it?

Question to self: "If speaking is the way for me to go, how do I make a living at it in the short-term, so as to leave a legacy from it in the long-term? How do I do it?"

I took action and got in touch with a number of professional speakers, asking for guidance and advice. I also followed up on some previously perused websites of speakers' bureaus and conference planners. My most serious inquiries were made to four seminar companies.

I was making lots of casts but getting no bites. This would've been the time in the past when the internal parrots would start to jabber. This time they remained silent a little longer.

It is easier to venture out when the voices are silent.

On Wednesday April 18, 2001, I got both a nibble and a rejection.

When picking up the mail, I honed in on a letter from one of the seminar companies, to which I had submitted my speaker promo package. The letter was opened and read before I'd even made it back to the house, a journey of not more than forty paces: "Thank you for your inquiry about speaking opportunities at Seminars R Us. We have received a number of applications and will be reviewing your résumé and video submission … blah blah blah … blah blah blah."

The real message: "Kindly go drown yourself."

In the short time it took me to get in the front door and climb the stairs to the upstairs office, the parrots of negativity were warming up their vocal cords. To shut them up I decided to call the other seminar companies, which I hadn't yet heard from.

The first call resulted in an abrupt, "Don't call us; we'll call you."

Squawk, said the lead parrot.

My second call resulted in an interminable journey through apparently endless voice mail.

Squawk, squawk, squawk, said the now trio of parrots.

One more call: voice mail, try again later. A half-hour later, same voice mail. Three more attempts, three more connections to nothing more than voice mail and the parrots were in full voice.

One last attempt I told myself. Bingo!

"What a coincidence that you should call. I just finished looking at your video not more than an hour ago. I was going to be contacting you in the next few days."

The speaker's tone was personable and genuine. Her bubbly style was most refreshing compared with what I was expecting. We chatted pleasantly for a couple of minutes and then she asked if I'd be interested in attending an audition.

"Interested? I'd crawl over broken glass."

She laughed. Good sign.

"When and where is the next audition?" I asked.

"Well, the very next one is next week, but that's all filled up. It'll be a couple of months until the one after that, which will be in Houston."

"Two months? Wow. That long? Where are the auditions next week? Maybe I could just turn up, in case there's a no-show."

"Next week is in Chicago. Hang on a minute."

She was gone for much more than a minute, allowing me to wonder what I would need to do for an audition. What would I talk about? What did they want? How would I get there? What do I do if I have to wait another eight weeks before I even get to an audition?

The parrots resumed their jabbering, making it hard for me to think.

"Sorry to keep you waiting, Ray. I'm trying to get a hold of the person who is running the show next week. Can you wait a little longer?"

"Sure. No problem."

This time she returned quickly.

"Okay, if you can make it to Chicago, we can fit you in before the scheduled auditions start at nine. What do you think? Can you make it?"

"You betcha!"

As I was about to hang up I heard myself say something eerily reminiscent of Peter Falk's character, Lieutenant Columbo.

"By the way, one last question: What do I do for the audition?"

"Whatever you like, Ray."

"Whatever I like?"

"Whatever you like."

"Can you narrow it down a little for me? What are they looking for in auditions?"

"Easy, Ray—sell me something."

"Sell you something?"

"You got it. Sell me something. Have a good weekend. See you Monday."

I sat there mystified, but then it was time to make a move. All righty, then! Chicago here I come.

I had three days to figure out how to sell them something, along with where to stay, how to get there, what to wear.

Four or five hours perusing six years of competition speeches was followed by three days of preparation and rehearsal. I decided to use the speech that had placed me second at the Toastmasters regional final two years earlier, adding a couple of extra minutes of content to satisfy the required "sell me something" injunction.

Getting to Chicago was to prove either expensive or arduous. Last-minute airfare, without the advance purchase discount or Saturday stay over, was a whopping two thousand bucks. Putting out two grand on nothing more than an audition long shot didn't seem to make much sense. Then again, Chicago was almost six hundred miles away and driving would take many hours. I decided that arduous was better than expensive.

On the lengthy drive on Sunday, I had ten hours to practice, practice, practice the speech, knowing that this ten-minute audition could be a turning point. Over and over again I went through the speech from beginning to end, changing inflection, emphasis, and timing. Les Brown, one of the all-time greats in the world of motivational speaking, was my driving companion. His booming, powerful voice on my CD player filled me with an optimism and enthusiasm of sizable proportions.

As I drifted off to sleep in a modest motel on the fringes of downtown Chicago, only minutes from the audition location, I was filled with an expectancy that was tempered with pragmatism.

FINDING YOUR WAY

- Means developing a resilient and determined ability to hear your own quiet voice of confidence over the roar of the negative voices of others.
- Is discovering your passion and trusting your instincts.
- Involves having honest conversations with yourself.
- Means taking action, any action; action is always better than inertia.
- Involves expecting the best and being prepared for the worst.
- Demands persistence, resilience, and determination.

"Nothing in the world can take the place of persistence. Talent will not; nothing is more common than unsuccessful men with talent. Genius will not; unrewarded genius is almost a proverb. Education will not; the world is full of educated derelicts. Persistence and determination alone are omnipotent …" — Calvin Coolidge

18

ACHIEVING
THE
DREAM

The speech was delivered to the motel bathroom mirror twice and then the mirrored closet door three times more. I arrived at the 37th floor of the office tower twenty minutes early and paced the hallway. It took strength of will not to compare this with the pacing, decades earlier, outside the inner sanctum of Mr. Pons.

At precisely 8:30 a.m. I entered the audition room and was greeted by the bubbly voice of last Wednesday's phone call. She was as charming in person as over the telephone. She directed me to fill in some paperwork and then led me into the audition room.

The room was set up with enough chairs for maybe a hundred people, the rows going wide and long. Bubbly voice introduced me to Deia Rank, director of faculty operations, a striking blonde with professional poise.

"Hello Ray, I'm Deia. Thank you for coming. You should know that we don't have contracts with us today and we will not be deciding on any speakers. There are several people waiting their turn in what is going to be a very busy schedule. You have ten minutes. Whenever you're ready."

Bubbly voice sat in the farthest chair, last row. Deia took the farthest chair, front row, on the opposite side.

Showtime!

The parrots were mute but the butterflies were airborne.

Zig Ziglar is credited with saying, "It isn't about getting rid of the butterflies. It's about getting the butterflies to fly in formation."

Mine were all over the place. To my relief, the moment I began to speak, they began to form up.

It was maybe the best delivery of any speech I had ever made: seamless, smooth, and flawless. Again, it's not bragging if it's the truth. As well as I thought the speech was going, the silence throughout the hall was worrisome. An audience of two provides minimal feedback. Sure, they did chuckle at the appropriate times and seemed to be engaged with my delivery. Nonetheless, it was hard to sense whether I was truly connecting.

My speech concluded with: "Dance, dance, dance ... dance, as if no one is watching."

Three seconds of silence that felt like three minutes, and then Deia jumped up, came toward me, and announced, "Ray, we need to talk." She turned to bubbly voice and instructed: "Tell them we'll be a little delayed."

Professional Deia became machine-gun-talker Deia. "I see you doing communication training, maybe a couple of the supervisor workshops or conflict management." Rat-a-tat-tat. "What do you think? Which workshops are you interested in? When are you available? We book three, four months in advance, so we probably wouldn't be able to book you in the next few weeks, but after that for sure. Did you get information on the pay structure? Where do you live? Is it close to a major airport?"

My turn to be gobsmacked.

Eight minutes later I left with a brochure for their two-day

Ultimate Communication Skills workshop and an assurance that they would be in touch soon. The twelve-hour drive home seemed much shorter than the ten-hour drive of the day before. "We'll be in touch soon. We'll be in touch."

I didn't hear squat for a full eight weeks. An agonizing eight weeks. During which time the parrot voices were putting on whole concerts in my head.

Then at last I received a call to book a one-week swing for September and another two weeks for later in the year. Some days later, the contract papers arrived and at last I was officially operational: "Professional Speaker."

It proved to be a full nineteen weeks from the audition before I would actually begin my practice of passion as a paid speaker. Nineteen weeks is not my idea of soon, and the delay had already made the change of career another roller-coaster ride of emotions.

Finally I donned the microphone on a sunny September Monday in Regina, Saskatchewan, day one of a two-day Management and Leadership Skills for First Time Managers and Supervisors, to be followed by the same seminar in Edmonton plus a tag day on Friday of Criticism and Discipline Skills.

My day began at six a.m. and the Kelly Temp assistant arrived at seven. There was to be a small group of only twenty-five people. I'd prepared long hours, over days, weeks, mostly seated in the garage, poring over the trainer notes and dissecting the workbook in microscopic detail. I was now a "Professional Speaker." Professionals prepare. Day one went quite nicely.

Day two found me back in the seminar room bright and early, continuing the planning for what I would do to conclude my first seminar on a festive note.

At eight thirty the first of the attendees arrived asking me if I had seen the news.

"No. Why do you ask?"

"A plane has flown into the World Trade Center."

"I've been to New York many times and with all the helicopters and aircraft traffic there, I'm surprised it hasn't happened before."

Have you ever said something totally boneheaded without realizing it?

"No, not a small plane, a passenger jet: terrorists, they think."

"What?"

We walked toward the lobby and noticed that hotel staff had turned on the big screen TV in the bar. Replays were being shown of American Airlines flight 11 crashing into the North Tower of the World Trade Center. Those horrifying images were followed by replays of United Airlines flight 175 doing the same to the South Tower.

My second day as a professional speaker was the day the world changed forever: September 11, 2001.

Not long before that tragic day, I had visited the observation deck of the World Trade Center. Both towers were now belching thick smoke into the Manhattan sky.

Then we learned that American flight 77 had crashed into the Pentagon and images of the gaping hole in the Pentagon building in D.C. were added to the news broadcasts. Later in the morning we learned of United Flight 93 crashing near Shanksville, Pennsylvania.

The world was gobsmacked and will forever be so.

Had this terrorist act taken place two years into my speaking career, I would most certainly have cancelled the day. Two days into my new adventure, that was never even contemplated.

Somehow we got through the seminar.

You will recall that all flights were grounded on that infamous Tuesday, making it impossible for me to make it to Edmonton that evening. Fortunately, I was able to secure the same hotel room for the night. I watched the horrific realities of 9/11 being played out on every TV channel. Along with the rest of the world I was glued to CNN, CBC, NBC, ABC, CTV, Fox, surfing from one network to another long into the night.

National Seminars had found a replacement speaker for the following day in Edmonton and faculty people were attempting to figure out what needed to be done next, as circumstances would allow.

Wednesday I rented a car and drove almost eleven hours through Saskatchewan into Edmonton, Alberta. Thursday morning I met Kit Grant, the replacement speaker, and sat through day two of the seminar watching a master at work. I'd met Kit at a Canadian Association of Professional Speakers conference in Calgary, not knowing that he had been a ten-year veteran speaker for National Seminars. He was no longer doing public training events; however, he was willing to fill in because of the special circumstances of 9/11.

Friday I finished off the week doing the tag-day of Criticism and Discipline Skills and was pleased to learn that I'd be able to fly home later in the day because the grounding of all flights had been lifted.

Security at the airport was extraordinary. Tension was palpable, nerves evident, patience non-existent. The normal white noise of an airport had changed to crackling tension. It was therefore surprising that I could hear my name being paged to "pick up any white courtesy phone for an outside call." Me? Paged in an airport? With the help of an Air Canada agent, I found my way to a phone and waited to be connected.

"Ray, Deia. I am so glad that I got a hold of you. How was your week?"

"Well, given what took place, my week worked out fine. How was yours?"

"You can imagine. Which is why I wanted to talk to you, Ray. We've got sixty-five people at a seminar in Winnipeg on Monday and we're not sure that our scheduled speaker will be able to make it from where he is currently stranded. We're also not certain that he or any of the U.S. speakers will be able to cross the border. We just don't know what's going on.

"Here's the thing," she continued. "We were hoping that you might be able to substitute for him and do the seminars on Monday and Tuesday next week in Winnipeg. Are you available?"

"Well, I do have a weekend golf tournament, but hey, in the circumstances, yes, I'm available. What's the seminar?"

"Collecting Accounts Receivable."

"Say again?"

"Collecting Accounts Receivable."

"That's what I thought you said, Deia. But listen to me: I know nothing, absolutely nothing, about collecting receivables. Are you sure you want me to do this?"

"Ray, we really aren't looking for you to do anything more than stop the people from walking out. Just put on the seminar and avoid too many of the attendees from fleeing the event. I know we're asking a lot. If you could do it I would be very appreciative."

"Well, okay, sure, I'll do my best."

My weekend golf tournament with the Lumpin' Cup boys had to be canceled. This is a group of twenty, twenty-four guys who gather together once a year to play some of the most serious rules–compliant golf ever played by a bunch of amateurs and then do some even more serious drinking. Golfers travel in from all over Ontario as well as Scotland and California. It felt criminal to cancel. But didn't everyone have their 9/11 stories, involving little or large sacrifices? I guess this was mine.

For eight hours on Saturday I was on the phone with another National Seminars speaker, Lisa Mackenzie, as she guided me through the Collecting Accounts Receivables program. This Mrs. Mackenzie was a heck of a lot more encouraging than the earlier one. Nevertheless, it was arduous, mind-numbing work.

The Saturday effort was followed by another three and a half hours on Sunday morning before I headed out to the airport.

Even with all the hours on the phone, and multiple reassurances from Lisa that I would do just fine, I wasn't feeling any great optimism.

FINDING YOUR WAY

- Means never losing focus on the bigger issues that matter most.
- Can involve great opportunity wrapped up in great tragedy.
- Is doing all you can do.

All You Can Do Is All You Can Do but All You Can Do Is Enough! — Title of book by A.L. Williams

19

ADVERSITY
POINTS
THE
WAY

The setting was the Holiday Inn South, Pembina Highway, Winnipeg. Sixty-eight people were in attendance at the seminar, all of them eager to gain more know-how for converting overdue debts into cash payments. The program coordinator working with me was a lady with a sour disposition. If my optimism wasn't that high before meeting her, it certainly didn't improve after.

So what? "All you can do is all you can do but all you can do is enough." It was time for me to do all I could do.

There are a variety of ways that the effectiveness of a public seminar speaker is measured. The key factors are evaluation scores, money-backs, and per cap. At this event, two of the factors didn't matter much. The National Seminars folks were expecting, and prepared to accept, less than great evaluations and lofty per caps. The only legitimate requirement had been stated by Deia when asking me to conduct the seminar: "Avoid too many people fleeing the event." In other words, minimize the money-backs.

The National Seminars folks were also expecting and prepared to accept that some of the collection professionals would see through my lack of experience and ask for a refund of their registration fees. As long as there weren't too many.

You would think that the pressure I felt to perform would therefore be less. It wasn't.

No matter how stumpy other people's expectations might be, the only expectation that truly matters is the one you place on yourself. It therefore didn't concern me that Deia would settle for mediocrity. I was striving to focus in on a much more positive approach. "Go big or go home! Give it all you got. Hoo-hah!"

Then the negatives chimed in: "Yeah right, hotshot. Get real. You don't know what you're talking about. Collecting Accounts Receivables? Prepare all you want, Raymondo, but there's no substitute for knowledge, substance, and credibility."

I wanted to do awesome, while feeling gruesome. What if all you can do is not enough? It can put you in a real pickle. But when in a pickle, stop thinkin'—start actin'.

You have no doubt had days when the odds are severely stacked against you. But there are also days when Jupiter aligns with Mars and the universe unfolds just as you feel it should. This was one of those days.

Minimum standard for evaluation scores is 5.2 out of 6. Winnipeg attendees gave me 5.5. Money-backs are typically required to be less than one percent. For this event I'm guessing they would have been pleased if refunds weren't more than maybe ten percent. Money-backs were in fact zero. Not one single attendee asked for a refund. No one fled. And perhaps the most startling number of all was the per cap. This is the product sales for the day divided by the people in attendance to arrive at the per person ratio. Expectation is $15. Doing well would be $30. That day in Manitoba we got $65. Sixty-five magnificent dollars! Wow.

Day two was a smaller group of forty-five people with an evaluation score of 5.4, again no money-backs, and a per cap of $50.

Never in my wildest dreams had I envisaged these kinds of numbers.

Prior to 9/11, I had three weeks of work booked out with National Seminars. Magically, three more weeks were added to the itinerary for 2001, and 2002 saw me on the road for forty-one weeks, delivering fifteen different topics and earning a six-figure income—admittedly at the very lowest end of the six-figure scale, but six figures all the same.

While the speaking industry was taking a huge hit and many speakers were experiencing significant reductions in income, here I was, at the very beginning of my speaking career, fresh out of the starting gate yet reaping immediate, sizeable rewards.

Even the most tragic, most horrific, most merciless of events can provide some positive impact.

FINDING YOUR WAY

- Sometimes requires, demands, that you find a way to get through challenge, tragedy, and catastrophe.
- Is possible even in the darkest and most difficult of times.
- Demands that you give it all you've got.

"I believe life is constantly testing us for our level of commitment, and life's greatest rewards are reserved for those who demonstrate a never-ending commitment to act until they achieve. This level of resolve can move mountains, but it must be constant and consistent. As simplistic as this may sound, it is still the common denominator separating those who live their dreams from those who live in regret." — Anthony Robbins

20

LEAVE
A
LEGACY

Since that time, it has been my privilege to travel across Canada and the U.S. delivering workshops, seminars, and on-site presentations for National Seminars, as well as delivering keynote speeches in my own right at conferences, meetings, and conventions.

More recently, with Queen Bee as CEO, we have established The Growth Coach, Newmarket, Ontario, which provides coaching services to business owners, entrepreneurs, and self-employed men and women who want to grow their businesses and balance their lives.

Life right now is about as good as it has ever been. I live a blessed existence. I give thanks each day, more than once, for the abundance that I receive every day.

Perhaps my biggest learning from the experiences over the years is to never take business or life for granted. Don't get too high when things are good and don't get too low when things don't go the way you would like.

Will I experience ups and downs in business? Turbulent times in life? Undoubtedly! Will there be times that I get the FUDs—fears, uncertainties, doubts—and need to silence the jabbering parrots? You betcha! Will the path ahead sometimes wind, meander, twist, and turn? Probably. In fact, I hope so. Life lived in a predictable, linear manner would be boring and monotonous. All of business and all of life is an unpredictable, exciting adventure. I encourage you, urge you, to fully live in the present and never, ever give up on finding your way to a better tomorrow. Find your way. Leave a legacy.

On that point, allow me to introduce you to my dad.

My dad was an uneducated man. He was born in an age when you left school at around fourteen years of age and went to work. Some years after leaving school, he joined the Royal Air Force and went off to war to do his duty for King and country.

He never owned his own business.

He never owned his own home.

He was never elected to office, never held a position of importance, never enjoyed status, power, or influence.

He didn't sit on any important committees and wasn't prominent in politics, business, or society.

He died at an alarmingly early age, fifty-three, having lived every week of his far too short life going from paycheck to paycheck.

Yet twenty-five years after his death, when Queen Bee and I visited the British Legion where he would go for a pint on a Saturday night, people were talking about him still.

Never, ever doubt your ability to make a meaningful impact on the world: to leave a footprint, to leave a lasting memory, to leave a legacy.

Extraordinary impact is being made every moment of every day by ordinary people. It is not only the anointed leaders of this world who were born to greatness. This book has been about you and me recognizing, discovering, and unleashing our greatness and leaving a powerful, enduring legacy of our own on this planet.

Let's do it now.

There has never been a better time than now, this instant, this very moment, to recognize, embrace, and engage in finding your way and leaving a legacy. My dad did it. If my dad can do it, I can do it. And if I can do it, you sure as shootin' can do it, too.

To your success!

- Fulfills your ultimate potential.
- Maps out a path for others.
- Leaves a legacy.

"Our worst fear is not that we are inadequate. Our deepest fear is that we are powerful beyond measure. It is our light, not our darkness, that frightens us. We ask ourselves: who am I to be brilliant, gorgeous, talented, or fabulous? Actually, who are you not to be? You are a child of God. Your playing small does not serve the world. And as we let our light shine, we unconsciously give other people permission to do the same. As we are liberated from our own fears our presence automatically liberates others." — Marianne Williamson

"We are not human beings having a spiritual experience. We are spiritual beings having a human experience." —Teilhard de Chardin

Parting Thought

The very best of your humanity, the most perfect way for you, which is worth searching for, finding, and following, cannot be reached by knowledge, nature, or laws of man alone.

Finding your way can only be discovered by aligning yourself with God and your divine God-given endowments.

You significantly increase your probability factor of finding your way when you focus on universal principles and fully harness the God-given powers that reside within.

Finding your way is leaving a legacy.

Finding your way is finding your greatness and then helping others to find their greatness.

Finding your way requires the power of God, the Source, Divine Power, Creator, Supreme Being, however you define your understanding of your God.

Finding your way is never easy; it is always worth it.

God bless you.

— Ray Pons

About the Author

Ray Pons was born in Southport, a seaside town near Liverpool, England, and now lives in Newmarket, Ontario, with his wife Marva Castillo (aka Queen Bee).

They have a daughter, Patricia, who is married to Ruddy, and a son Darien.

Ray is a lifelong fan of Liverpool FC, the "greatest football team of all time," and he is an avid if not terribly talented golfer.

In addition to being a keynote speaker on issues of Leadership, Interpersonal Excellence, and Life Balance, Ray is co-owner with Marva of The Growth Coach, Newmarket, which helps business owners, entrepreneurs, and self-employed men and women dramatically grow their businesses and achieve greater joy, freedom, and fulfillment in their lives.

To contact Ray about keynote speaking, training, or coaching services, e-mail him at ray@raypons.com.

www.raypons.com
www.thegrowthcoach.ca

9 780980 923131